IRELAND

Text by ELISABETTA CANORO

THUNDER BAY
P·R·E·S·S
San Diego, California

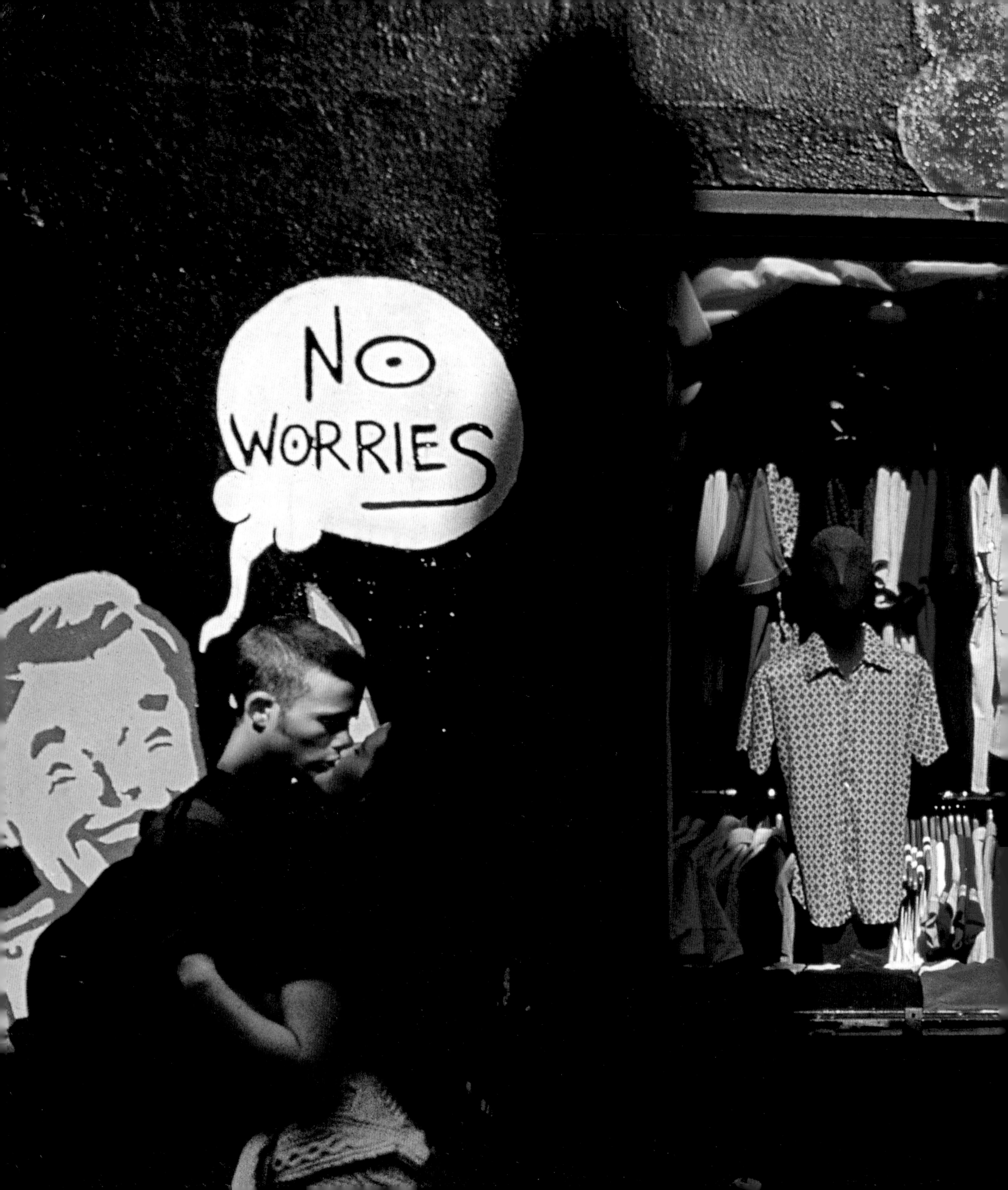
NO WORRIES

EDITORIAL PROJECT
Valeria Manferto De Fabianis

GRAPHIC DESIGN
Clara Zanotti

GRAPHIC REALIZATION
Clara Zanotti
Paola Piacco
Patrizia Balocco Lovisetti

EDITORIAL COORDINATION
Giada Francia

6-7 Many Aran islanders are fishermen; they have followed their calling for centuries in the local boats known as *currachs* or *curraghs*.

8 LEFT Fox hounds being trained while waiting for the season to open.

8 RIGHT Pale skin, freckles, and red hair are the typical Irish complexion.

8-9 The bright colors of a mural form the backdrop to a children's game in the streets of Kinvarra.

1 A young Irishman smiling behind the front door of his house in Listowel (or Lios Thuethail), a few miles to the south of the vast Shannon estuary.

2-3 The latest trends burst into the 16th-century Temple Bar, Dublin's artists' quarter.

4-5 Dotted with grazing sheep and straw bales, the peaceful countryside of St. John's Point extends out into Dundrum Bay, at the southern tip of County Down.

CONTENTS

11 Dublin's most elegant Georgian houses are to be seen in Merrion Square.

12-13 A hurling match in 1950: Two teams of 15 players compete for goals and points in this traditional display of speed and skill.

14-15 Mutakarrim, seen here jumping during the Galway Races, is one of the heroes of Irish steeplechasing, the specialty of Irish hunters born and bred in Ireland.

INTRODUCTION

THE MAGIC AND BEAUTY OF THE GREEN ISLAND

IRELAND IS "LIKE A SECOND HOME, A PLACE WE GO BACK TO AS SOON AS POSSIBLE."

THAT IS WHAT YOU OFTEN HEAR FROM VISITORS WHO INVARIABLY FALL IN LOVE WITH THE IRISH COUNTRYSIDE, AND WITH THE GOOD CHEER AND HOSPITALITY OF ITS INHABITANTS.

IRELAND IS A COUNTRY "SUSPENDED IN TIME," STILL BEARING MANY TRACES OF A DIFFICULT PAST BUT IN CONTINUAL TRANSFORMATION AND DEVELOPMENT. LOOKING TOWARD THE FUTURE WITH OPTIMISM AND FAITH IN HERSELF, IRELAND IS ATTEMPTING TO LEAVE HER TROUBLED HISTORY BEHIND: A HISTORY OF INVASIONS, A STRUGGLE FOR INDEPENDENCE, AND INTERNECINE WARS THAT HAVE MARKED HER LIFE AND PEOPLE. BUT THE IRISH ARE PROUD PEOPLE WHO HAVE NOT SHOWN SIGNS OF WEAKNESS; THEY HAVE ALWAYS RISEN AFRESH FROM DIFFICULTIES AND TURMOIL.

IRELAND IS A COUNTRY "SUSPENDED IN SPACE," WHERE THE VISITOR CANNOT HELP BUT BE STRUCK BY THE COUNTRYSIDE'S ENDLESS GREEN EXPANSES AND GENTLE SILENCE. THE ISLAND'S COASTS ARE ROUGH AND JAGGED, ALIVE WITH THE VITALITY AND ROAR OF THE SEA. AND THE SKY IS ALWAYS CHANGING, WITH HUES THAT BLEND WITH THOSE OF THE ATLANTIC.

IRELAND IS A COUNTRY OF A THOUSAND COLORS, PAINTED WITH ALL THE POSSIBLE TONES OF A FULL PALETTE, A SMALL COUNTRY BUT WITH AN EXTRAORDINARY VARIETY OF LANDSCAPES.

THE NATION IS ONE OF THE LAST BULWARKS OF THE OLD CONTINENT FACING OUT TO THE ATLANTIC. A STRONGHOLD SURROUNDED BY THE SEA AND PROTECTED BY TRUSTY SENTINELS — HER LIGHTHOUSES — JUST AS THOUGH IRELAND WERE HERSELF A LIGHTHOUSE THAT PROTECTS THE REST OF EUROPE.

IN SHORT, IRELAND IS A PLACE THAT WILL AFFECT YOU, THAT YOU WILL RESPOND TO. HER BEAUTY AND MAGIC ARE CREATED NOT JUST BY HER ENDLESS NATURAL VISTAS, BUT ALSO BY THE LEGENDS, MYTHS, AND HISTORY THAT HAVE SHAPED THE PAST OF THIS PEOPLE, AS WELL AS THE LITERATURE, TRADITIONS, MUSIC, AND CINEMA THAT CHARACTERIZE THE PRESENT.

IN IRELAND IT IS IMPOSSIBLE NOT TO BE DRAWN IN BY THE CHEERFULNESS, THE ENJOYMENT OF BEING ALIVE, AND BY THE WARMTH OF THE IRISH, WHO GATHER IN PUBS AND STREETS TO DRINK, SING, AND DANCE. IT IS A "SUNNY" COUNTRY THAT NEVER LOSES HOPE.

A COUNTRY WHERE IT OFTEN RAINS BUT WHERE SUNSHINE ALWAYS RETURNS.

CONTESTED CHRONICLES

THE DAWN OF IRISH CIVILIZATION

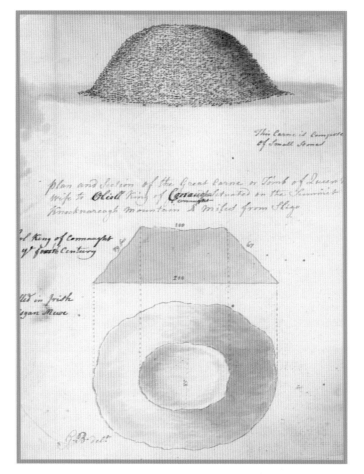

The agricultural settlers who inhabited Ireland during the Neolithic Age (circa 4000 to 2000 B.C.) gave rise to a mysterious Irish civilization that lasted thousands of years and left 1,500 burial sites scattered throughout the country. The finest examples are the large Brugh na Boinne necropolis (the Newgrange, Knowth, and Dowth tumuli) in the Boyne Valley and the Carrowmore Megalithic Cemetery, near Sligo, which, with around forty dolmens and portal tombs, is the country's largest array of Stone Age burial places.

Many other archaeological sites predate 4000 B.C. In most cases, these are the remains of dwellings dating back as far as 7000 B.C., associated with Mesolithic Age hunter-gatherers. They had left Britain, crossed the Irish Sea, and settled in Ireland's southern and western areas.

A significant turning point in early Irish civilization came in about 1500 B.C., when the Gaeli, a Celtic tribe from Central Europe, reached the coast of Ireland. This was hardly a true invasion, as the Gaeli arrived in a trickle rather than a stream, but the hundred or so tiny chiefdoms, or *tuatha,* into which the island was eventually divided are testimony to the fact that the new civilization fully colonized the country. The chiefdoms existed within the Five Fifths — the five provinces of Meath, Leinster, Munster, Connaught, and Ulster. A population of warriors, priests, and poets, the Celts lived in isolated rural communities. They conducted their daily lives according to an extremely ancient system of laws, later codified as the Brehon Law, worshipped numerous deities, and loyally obeyed their sovereigns. Each chiefdom was headed by a chieftain, with the *Ard Righ,* or High King, exercising overall power from his throne in the Hill of Tara in County Meath. Significant power was also wielded by the Druids, the priests who, as well as performing religious duties, were judges, genealogists, historians, and poets.

The exceptional artistic talents of this population deserve particular mention; archaeologists have found numerous high-quality gold, silver, and bronze artifacts from the period. The warriors, in particular, were fervent collectors of jewelry: necklaces, *torcs* (strips of twisted gold or bronze), collars, stones, fibulae, and sword hilts bearing the sophisticated decoration of the central European La Tène culture.

Celtic civilization has left no written evidence. The only known form of Irish Celtic writing is the little-used linear Ogham script found on the so-called Ogham Stones in the form of magical or commemorative inscriptions.

The most illustrious chieftains were remembered through stories of their valor that, through oral retelling, inspired generation after generation. The epic cycles involving Cúchulainn and Fionn Mac Cumhaill, fearless, indomitable heroes whose feats remain cloaked in magic and myth, have survived to the present day.

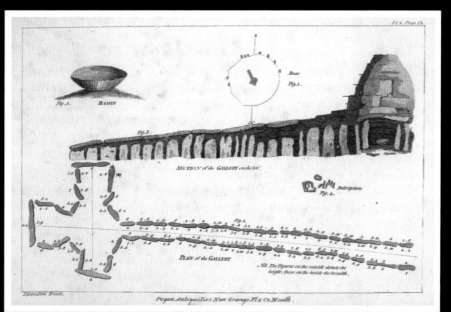

20 THE *BOOK OF KELLS*, CREATED AROUND 800 A.D., IS A MAGNIFICENT ILLUMINATED MANUSCRIPT WITH RICHLY DECORATED PAGES LIKE THIS ONE DEPICTING ST. MATTHEW. THE BOOK IS NOW AT TRINITY COLLEGE, DUBLIN, AND IS CONSIDERED A JEWEL IN THE COLLEGE'S LIBRARY COLLECTIONS.

21 LEFT AND RIGHT FURTHER EXAMPLES OF THE COMPLEX DECORATION OF THE *BOOK OF KELLS*. THE MANUSCRIPT CONTAINS THE TEXT OF THE FOUR GOSPELS IN LATIN.

The line lengthens in the courtyard of Trinity College, Dublin, a location that appears to have emerged directly from the script of *The Dead Poets Society*. Beyond the threshold, in a darkened library hall, an illuminated manuscript glitters. This is the *Book of Kells,* one of the most beautiful manuscripts ever created. Behind this masterpiece of intricate medieval art lies the great Irish monastic civilization, which represents one of the most significant religious and cultural triumphs of western Christianity. The new faith came to Ireland in about the fifth century. The seventh and eighth centuries, the Dark Ages of medieval Europe, coincided with the construction of the great Irish monasteries inhabited by monks devoted to creating illuminated manuscripts and committed to spreading the Christian religion. The proliferation of these sites was due above all to Ireland's deep interior and

a belief (unfortunately misplaced) in its natural impregnability that led to its adoption as a safe haven by the religious orders.

In all probability, the *Book of Kells* was the work of the monks of Iona who sought refuge at Kells, County Meath, in 806 after a Viking invasion of their remote island home off the southwest Scottish coast. The famous manuscript contains the texts of the Four Gospels written in Latin. What makes it unique are the elaborate interlaced motifs and the animal and human figures that decorate its pages.

Today, it is still possible to visit and admire the early monastic centers at Clonmacnoise in County Offaly, Glendalough in County Wicklow, and Devenish Island in County Fermanagh. Other religious buildings meriting a visit include those at Gallarus in County Kerry, Clonfert in County Galway, and the Rock of Cashel in County Tipperary.

22 ST. PATRICK CONVERTS AN IRISH KING. THE PATRON SAINT OF IRELAND WAS A COMPELLING PREACHER WHO SUCCEEDED IN SPREADING CHRISTIANITY THROUGHOUT THE COUNTRY.

23 ST. BRENDAN, A MISSIONARY MONK AND SKILLED SEAMAN, SAILED TO DISTANT LANDS ABOARD A *CURRAGH* (A TRADITIONAL BOAT PROPELLED BY A SAIL AND OARS). HE HAD TO COPE WITH UNTOLD DANGERS DURING HIS VOYAGES.

The religious history of Ireland is in the sites associated with the early Church and in the records of the saints and missionaries who preached the gospel far beyond the nation's borders. St. Patrick, St. Brendan, St. Columba, St. Finnian, St. Columbanus, St. Gall, St. Colman, St. Frigidian, St. Cathaldus, and St. Donatus — these are the best loved exemplars of this heroic history, men who sailed the seas to evangelize distant lands. Once arrived, they worked to convert pagan peoples and found new monasteries and abbeys. Their lives and their adventurous journeys are recounted in stories and legends in which reality and fantasy are frequently confused. True or not, these stories have become an integral part of the spirituality and culture of the Irish people; they recognize and revere the religious figures who made decisive contributions to the Christianization of the country. Their fame, bolstered by the faith and devotion of an entire population, transcends national and temporal borders.

St. Patrick's Day (March 17), honoring Ireland's most famous saint, confirms the foregoing claim: It is celebrated not only in Ireland but throughout the globe, from Dublin to New York to Sydney. The patron saint of Ireland and a central figure in Celtic Christianity, St. Patrick lived in the fifth century. He was not a native Irishman but was born in a tiny village in Scotland, not far from Glasgow, in the Kilpatrick hills near Dumbarton. Much of what we know about him comes from his own writings. One of these is his *Confessio,* a text contained in *The Book of Armagh,* a ninth-century codex conserved at Trinity College. From this text we learn that at the age of sixteen he was kidnapped by Irish pirates during one of their raids and sold to a shepherd as a pig herder. Having landed in the Skerries promontory to the northeast of Dublin, Patrick spent six long years as a slave on Slemish Mountain. Finally he managed to escape and return to Britain. There he had a dream in which God revealed Patrick's mission to him: He was to convert the very people who had enslaved him. After preparing for the priesthood in various monasteries in France and Italy, Patrick returned to Ireland as a bishop in about 432. He wandered the length and breadth of the country, aided the needy, founded monasteries and abbeys, preached, and performed remarkable miracles such as the banishing of snakes from the island. He was distinguished by his persuasiveness as a preacher and his ability to convert both ordinary people and men of power, such as King Angus. St. Patrick persuaded this monarch to embrace Christianity on the Rock of Cashel that, tradition has it, rose on a rock spat out by the devil because the saint was building a great church on the plain below. Over a period of about thirty years, Patrick converted virtually the entire population of Ireland. According to the legend, he died at the age of 120 and was buried at Down (known since as Downpatrick) in Ulster. Another great Irish saint, St. Columbanus, was responsible for the foundation of no fewer than fifty-three monasteries known as the *familiae Columbae*, whose member monasteries were run according to the rules and in keeping with spirit of the saint. During the sixth century, St. Brigid established Ireland's first monastery for women in Kildare. In reality, very little is known about St. Brigid, and those who attempt to reconstruct and record her life have to place considerable faith in the imaginative legends in which she appears. Of all the Irish missionary saints, the one who traveled farthest was St. Brendan, a native of the Clonfert region. An accomplished sailor, he was very skilled in the handling of the *curragh*, a typical small boat with a sail and oars and a leather-clad hull. These craft were used to cover long distances and to brave the ocean storms. According to some sources, toward the end of the fifth century, Brendan decided to attempt to cross the Atlantic and, if the body of legend is to be believed, actually reached America a full millennium before Christopher Columbus. Particular mention should also be made of St. Columbanus who was responsible for the introduction of individual confessions rather than the collective confession practiced previously. He is also attributed with the founding of monasteries in France, Switzerland, Germany, Austria, and in Italy, at Bobbio, where he personally contributed to the building of the church and monastery and where he died in 615.

24 LEFT The swift, light *drakkar* with its elongated, dragonlike hull was the vessel used by Viking invaders who landed in Ireland around 800 and subsequently headed toward the European mainland.

24 RIGHT While fighting the king of Connaught, Dermot MacMurrough, King of Leinster, called upon the Earl of Pembroke for aid. The Earl, having recruited an army of Norman soldiers from northern France, landed at Baginbun on Ireland's southeastern coast.

THE INVASIONS: THE VIKINGS AND THE NORMANS

The first Viking ships were sighted off the verdant coastlines of northern and eastern Ireland in the second half of the eighth century. To be precise, the first raid took place in 795. From that date on, the Vikings returned on numerous occasions and in ever-increasing numbers. The term "raid" is appropriate in this context as the Viking conquest of Ireland was by no means peaceful. Having landed, the invaders usually laid waste to everything in their path. They attacked the settlements, sacked and burned the monasteries, and spread terror among the population. Fearsome warriors, the Vikings brought into Ireland a civilization founded on martial values.

A new phase of conquest commenced from the ninth century onward as the Vikings began to settle in the country in large numbers and to establish alliances with the local people. During this period they built a number of fortified settlements, generally at the mouths of the rivers. This practice gave rise to towns such as Wexford, Waterford, Wicklow, Youghal, Cork, Bantry, Limerick and the capital itself, Dublin. However, this situation was not to remain stable for long. The uneasy cohabitation between the Vikings and the native Irish people continued to be difficult — and the invaders were destined for eventual defeat. The decisive blow was struck in the Battle of Clontarf in 1014. Here Brian Ború, the old king of Munster, led the Irish to victory, though he was killed while the Vikings were actually retreating. Unfortunately, loss of the authoritative figurehead and internal divisions among the Irish tribal leaders prevented this victory over the invaders from leading to the birth of a solid, unitary kingdom.

The Vikings who remained in the country, however, proved to be capable of integrating with the native people. They converted to Christianity and fought alongside the Irish during the struggles against the next invaders, the Normans.

This phase in Irish history began in 1066, when William the Conqueror and his Normans invaded and

24-25 In 1169, Anglo-Norman forces invaded Ireland, conquering Dublin, Wexford, and Waterford.

26 The Anglo-Irish colonists made extensive use of cavalry to take over what became their lands and to subsequently defend them.

27 LEFT During the Irish campaign, the English troops, led by King Richard II, were supplied by sea.

27 RIGHT The king of Leinster gallops up to the duke of Gloucester, dispatched by King Richard II of England to negotiate with the Irish.

27 BOTTOM Edward III, King of England (1312–1377).

seized England. Initially, neighboring Ireland did not appear to be of any interest to the Normans, but, unfortunately, it was only a question of time until it would, and paradoxically it was an Irish leader who attracted the Normans' attention. The spark for the onset of hostilities was provided by a woman; no ordinary woman, of course, but none other than the wife of Tiernan O'Rourke, king of Connaught, who had been kidnapped by Dermot MacMurrough, the king of Leinster. In actual fact, it is by no means certain there was a true kidnapping; it is rather more likely that she followed MacMurrough of her own accord. Naturally, the relationship between the two bitter enemies hardly improved after this episode, and O'Rourke eventually got the better of his rival. Having fled abroad in search of foreign allies, MacMurrough secured the support of Richard FitzGilbert de Clare, Earl of Pembroke (in Wales), better known as Strongbow. He in exchange requested the hand of Mac-Murrough's daughter in marriage, thereby ensuring his succession to MacMurrough's throne after the latter's death. It was thus that in 1169 the first Anglo-Norman forces landed in Bannow Bay, County Wexford. During the course of a year they conquered Wexford, Dublin, and Waterford. After MacMurrough's

death Strongbow succeeded him as king of Leinster and consolidated his position in Ireland.

At this point, Henry II of England could no longer ignore the situation. Strongbow was, after all, one of his subjects, even though it appeared that, along with the noblemen he had taken with him, he was day by day increasing his independence from the English Crown and royal authority. Henry II therefore decided to assemble a powerful naval force and set sail for Ireland. In 1171 he landed at Waterford, which he nominated a royal city. He had earlier secured the support of Pope Adrian IV, ironically the only Englishman ever to be elected to the papal throne.

Over the following two centuries, the descendants of these first Anglo-Norman settlers in Ireland became integrated within the existing social fabric. As a reaction to this state of affairs, Edward III of England attempted to reassert royal authority and in 1366 instituted the Statutes of Kilkenny, which severely prohibited mixed marriages and the use of the Irish language and customs. However, an irreversible process had been set in motion, and thanks to the strenuous resistance of the Irish people, English control over the country dwindled to the point where it was effectively restricted to the so-called Pale, a small area around Dublin.

THE PROTESTANT CONQUEST

In the fifteenth century Ireland's most powerful Anglo-Norman family, the FitzGeralds of Kildare, reinforced its position in the country. Initially, England's monarchy (now the Tudor dynasty) appeared to be unconcerned, with Henry VIII maintaining a policy of prudent disengagement. The situation was overturned with the opening of a schism between the English Crown and the Roman Catholic Church, which led to the first moves toward establishing a Protestant church in England. Henry VIII confiscated the wealthy Irish monasteries and assumed the title of king of Ireland, and in 1541 obliged the Irish parliament to crown him. Naturally, this worsened the already strained relationship between the local Anglo-Norman dynasties and the Irish clans. War broke out in the summer of 1534 and dragged on to 1540, the year in

which the FitzGeralds finally submitted to the authority of the English Crown. Subsequently, Henry VIII officially became the head of the church in Ireland, with the Dublin parliament passing a series of laws that recognized Henry's Act of Supremacy, approved by the English parliament in 1534. This led to the establishment of a three-pronged social structure: the Old English who swore loyalty to the king (without, however, recognizing his spiritual supremacy), the independent Irish Catholics, and the new Protestants, many of whom had obtained material benefits through the acquisition of ecclesiastical properties. During the reign of Henry VIII's daughter, Elizabeth I (1558–1603), England strengthened its hold over Ireland. For many English colonists the desire to spread the Protestant religion became a pretext for sup-

pressing the native Irish culture, religion, and language. This policy resulted in at least three major revolts by the Irish people. The first two, led by the Desmonds of Munster, were easily quelled with the confiscated lands being redistributed among the English colonists. The third that broke out in Ulster and was led by Hugh O'Neill was more serious and gave rise to the Nine Years' War (1594–1603). Initially protected by the English Crown, O'Neill rebelled when he realized he was actually nothing more than a pawn in the service of English Protestantism. The early stages of the revolt appeared to go his way and he actually enjoyed a major victory in the Battle of the Yellow Ford in 1598. However, in 1601, the English troops had the better of the Battle of Kinsale, and the collapse of O'Neill's power and the freedom of Ulster were in sight. In 1603, without knowing that Queen Elizabeth had died only a few days earlier, O'Neill signed the Treaty of Mellifont. The agreement ratified the House of Tudor's irreversible conquest of Ireland. In 1607, having lost any vestige of authority, O'Neill and a further ninety Ulster leaders chose permanent exile from Ireland and embarked en masse for continental Europe, a migration that was to go down in history as the Flight of the Earls. The English confiscated something in the region of half a million acres of Irish land, including the possessions of O'Neill himself. Having been relieved of the inconvenient presence of the local leaders, Elizabeth I's successor, James I, now had a free hand to actuate the policy of colonization known as the Plantation of Ireland. Basically, this involved the parceling out of land in the form of fortified properties to the numerous English and Scottish Protestant colonists, or "Undertakers," who had soon begun to arrive from the mainland. In this way, the English Crown could count on loyal settlements throughout Ireland. Moreover, the organization of these new colonies was managed directly by financially involved English corporations. Naturally, discontent among the Irish grew and, above all in Ulster, the division between Catholics and Protestants became irreparable.

30 In 1653, after the English Civil War and the execution of Charles I (1649), Oliver Cromwell assumed the title of Lord Protector of England, Scotland, and Ireland.

31 In September 1649, Cromwell's troops attacked the town of Drogheda, massacring thousands of people.

OLIVER CROMWELL AND THE ACT OF SETTLEMENT

The leader of the English parliamentary forces, Oliver Cromwell (who governed Britain from 1649–1660) is sadly famous for the ruthless campaign he conducted in Ireland. Landing on the island with 12,000 troops of the New Model Army, the anti-Catholic Cromwell reached Dublin in August 1649. In September he razed the city of Drogheda, killing thousands of men, women, and children.

He then headed south and in rapid succession occupied Wexford and New Ross. It was then the turn of Cork, Youghal, and Kinsale to capitulate swiftly, with the last bastion of Irish resistance to be conquered being Waterford. By the end of the war two years later, the Irish Catholic population had been reduced by a quarter. Under the Act of Settlement of 1652, vast tracts of Irish land were confiscated, with the inhabitants exiled to the inhospitable areas of western Ireland.

The process lasted a number of months, and many of the older and weaker exiles died en route. The confiscated lands were given to those members of Cromwell's army who settled in the territory.

33 LEFT A portrait of William of Orange (1650–1702) painted by Sir Godfrey Kneller in 1689.

33 RIGHT The day after his defeat in the Battle of the Boyne, James II fled to France.

JAMES II AND THE BATTLE OF THE BOYNE

In 1660, following Cromwell's death, the Stuart dynasty was restored in the person of Charles II. His accession to the throne reignited the hopes of the Irish Catholics, and in 1665 their position appeared to be further strengthened when Charles's pro-Catholic brother James II came to the throne. James appointed a Catholic viceroy to Ireland and effectively obtained the annulment of the Act of Settlement. In England, however, the Whigs and the Tories retaliated by offering the throne to the Protestant William of Orange (husband of King James's daughter Mary) who ruled as William III after James's deposition. Having lost his throne, James II sought refuge in Ireland, where he raised an army. The famous Battle of the Boyne in July 1690 proved to be the decisive encounter between the two kings: William III and the Protestants won a crushing victory over James and the Catholics. After this victory, William III proceeded to take concrete measures to consolidate Protestant control over Ireland.

34 LEFT Together with Henry Flood, Henry Grattan organized a strong "patriotic" party with the objective of improving the conditions and rights of Irish Catholics.

34 RIGHT The Irish Parliament met for the first time on April 16, 1782, in Dublin's House of Commons. It was then that Henry Grattan made Ireland's first declaration of independence.

FROM THE PENAL LAWS TO THE ACT OF UNION

In the early years of the eighteenth century, cohabitation of Ireland by the Catholic and Protestant factions became increasingly fraught. Within sixty years, the Protestant colonists (who accounted for around a tenth of the total population) had taken possession of virtually all Irish land, and the impoverished and embittered Catholics constituted a very real threat. In order to discourage Catholic insurrection, the Protestant noblemen had thus supported the passing of the infamous Penal Laws in the 1690s and thereafter, a body of legislation designed to suppress the Catholic population. Under these laws, the Catholics were disenfranchised and prohibited from enrolling in either the army or the navy. The Protestants also banned the Irish language and music, Catholic literature, and even the celebration of the mass. Educating children in the Catholic faith was outlawed. Catholics could neither buy nor inherit land; the only concession being allowed was the equal division of goods among all offspring. Rewards were actually offered to all those who decided to convert to Protestantism.

Underlying the Penal Laws was a clear determination to erase the identity, culture, and beliefs of the Irish people. Paradoxically, they had the opposite effect. Mass continued to be celebrated secretly, even when this meant holding services at night in the open countryside. Irish language and music were taught by outlaw teachers in clandestine open-air "hedge schools." All this helped keep the country's cultural heritage alive. It was not until after 1715 that the religious elements contained in the Penal Laws began to be applied less strictly.

In the late eighteenth century, Irish patriots became increasingly determined to end the worst discriminations against the Irish people and their traditional faith. A long struggle ensued. The ruling class in Ireland was solidly Protestant, made up of descendants of Cromwell's soldiers, English colonists from the Elizabethan age, and the Norman noblemen. In addition, the Irish parliament, composed entirely of Protestants, was obliged to subject any law it wished to pass to the British parliament and Crown for approval. For this reason Henry Grattan and Henry Flood founded the Patriotic Party, and Irish Protestants and Catholics joined forces to resist British influence over local issues. In the same period, the British empire's resources were committed to fighting the American War of Independence. In order to tackle the crisis, the majority of the British armed forces in Ireland were recalled and sent to fight in the American colonies. Ireland was left in the hands of Protestant "Volunteers" who were under the direct control of the landowners and merchants.

Fearing an Irish rebellion, the

35 **LEFT** Feverish preparations are underway for the last insurrection in favor of Irish independence. The rising, organized in Dublin in 1803 by Robert Emmet, was suppressed and Emmet was arrested and executed.

35 **RIGHT** In 1791 Theobald Wolfe Tone, a young Dublin lawyer, became a founding member of the United Irishmen, supporters of equal rights for Protestants and Catholics.

British government was now more inclined to make concessions, as demonstrated by the fact that in 1782 the so-called Grattan's Parliament (the Irish parliament meeting in Dublin) managed to obtain the legislative independence for Ireland. While the country was no longer under the yoke of the British parliament, there remained the matter of the royal veto. In 1783, with the Act of Renunciation, the British parliament formally "declared and assured for ever" the legislative independence of the Irish parliament, although in reality its independence was to last no longer than eighteen years.

With the outbreak of the French Revolution in 1789, groups of Protestant volunteers inspired by the great ideals of Liberty, Equality, and Brotherhood began to assemble throughout Ireland, determined to curb British power. One of these groups was the United Irishmen, founded in 1791 by Theobald Wolfe Tone, a young Protestant lawyer from Dublin who was convinced that independence from Britain had to be based on equal rights for Protestants and Catholics. Initially oriented toward a policy of nonviolence, the United Irishmen subsequently became a clandestine organization prepared to use all means, including force, to obtain change. In 1795, alarmed by the direction that events appeared to be taking, the Protestant Loyalists (loyal to the British Crown) founded the Protestant Orange Society, later to be known as the Orange Order. (The name harks back to William of Orange — William III of Great Britain — who in 1690 defeated the Catholic James II in the Battle of the Boyne.) The Irish government, feeling threatened by the United Irishmen and other similar Catholic groups that had on several occasions attempted to instigate rebellion, promoted a campaign to root out arms and the rebellious elements of the population. The indiscriminate flogging and torture that followed this decision led to the Insurrection of 1798. This was, however, an uncoordinated revolt and was bloodily suppressed. Wolfe Tone himself was arrested and taken to Dublin. Condemned to death, he preferred to take his own life before being executed. Following the rebellions culminating in the Insurrection of 1798, the British government in 1800 approved the Act of Union whereby Ireland legally became part of Great Britain. Coming into effect on January 1, 1801, the Act of Union put a definitive end to all hopes of an independent Ireland, at least until 1803, when Robert Emmet, a former member of the United Irishmen, organized a last attempt at insurrection in Dublin. While the revolt failed, with Emmet being captured, tried, and executed, it clearly demonstrated that the Irish rebel spirit had yet to be tamed.

36 LEFT THE POPULAR LEADER DANIEL O'CONNELL WAS THE SYMBOL OF NONVIOLENT STRUGGLE IN FAVOR OF CATHOLIC EMANCIPATION.

36 RIGHT THE TERRIBLE FAMINE THAT DEVASTATED IRELAND FROM 1845 TO 1851 CAUSED THE DEATHS OF ALMOST THREE MILLION PEOPLE.

DANIEL O'CONNELL, CHARLES STEWART PARNELL, AND THE LAND LEAGUE

Considered to be the "greatest popular leader history has ever known" and famously nicknamed "the Liberator," Daniel O'Connell (1775–1847) made Catholic emancipation through peaceful and legal means his life's work. The conviction that "liberty is not worth the shedding of one drop of blood" became the foundation of his political policy. The Catholic Association he founded in 1823 attracted a great number of followers, drawn to campaign for full political rights for the Catholic population. Such was his commitment and determination that in April 1829, King George IV approved the British parliament's Catholic Emancipation Act, which gave the vote to a limited number of Irish Catholics.

O'Connell's popularity and credibility continued to increase and in 1841 he was elected lord mayor of Dublin. Two years later he was involved in the ambitious project to repeal the Act of Union with Britain. At that time, huge crowds were attending the "monster meetings" that he held throughout Ireland. According to some estimates, over a million people — the equivalent of an eighth of the total population at that time — participated in one of his rallies staged on the Hill of Tara.

The English authorities believed they could undermine O'Con-

nell's influence by declaring the eagerly awaited Clontarf meeting of 1843 to be illegal. Keeping faith with his pacifist policy, O'Connell was obliged to cancel the event. Naturally, this cost him the support of certain sections of the population and paved the way to the eventual decline of power. The Irish political scene became dominated by movements that, in contrast to O'Connell's movement, claimed that armed struggle was the sole means of obtaining independence. One of these new groups was the Young Ireland movement. At first it was supportive of O'Connell's policy, but in 1848 it attempted an armed insurrection.

The Great Famine occurred during one of the most difficult periods of Ireland's history, adding immensely to the nation's sufferings and causing the deaths of many thousands of Irish peasants. Between 1800 and 1840, the country's population had risen from four to eight million. Poverty was widespread and most rural dwellers were feeding themselves almost exclusively on potatoes. The series of poor or almost nonexistent potato harvests between 1845 and 1849 had catastrophic consequences. With no hope of purchasing other products, not even the grain that was particularly abundant in that period, millions of people faced starvation. Paradoxically, while so many were dying of starvation at home, Irish produce continued to be exported overseas. The figures are horrifying: according to the estimates, between two and three million Irish people died of starvation and hardship in the seven-year period. For many thousands, the only alternative was emigration, usually to the promised land of America. But for many thousands even that was to remain a mirage; they were too poor, too old, or too weak to make the demanding voyage. Many others perished during the Atlantic crossing aboard overloaded ships, while still others died soon after embracing new hope on reaching Canada, the United States, Australia, and New Zealand. Overall, the mass emigration led to the creation of large Irish communities abroad, bringing an international dimension to the Irish people's struggle for independence.

Those who remained in Ireland gained a new sense of community, increasingly anti-British in feeling. During the famine, the general resentment felt toward the British government intensified, further fueled by the absentee British landlords' indifference to the sufferings of their Irish tenants.

Irish politics in the 1870s and 1880s was dominated by Charles Stewart Parnell, the restless and ambitious son of a Protestant landowner from Avondale in County Wicklow. Parnell was elected as a member of Parliament for County Meath and became the leader of the new Home Rule Party in 1877. It was his belief, in fact, that only a parliament located in Dublin could effectively respond to the local needs of the Irish people. He therefore concentrated his political activity on attempting to curb as far as possible the British parliament's authority over that of Ireland, and its interventions in Irish domestic affairs.

In 1879 the specter of famine again reared its head: On the one hand the potato harvest was disastrous, while on the other cheap grain from the United States was forcing down the price of that produced in Ireland. The obvious consequence was increased hardship for those tenant farmers who paid their rent out of the profits earned from grain. When large numbers of these farmers began to be evicted, Parnell and Michael Davitt founded the Land League.

Numerous revolts broke out in its name, with the aim of obtaining a reduction in rents and an improvement in working conditions. What came to be called the Land War lasted from 1879 through to 1882, with the tenant farmers eventually winning stronger rights, thereby tasting victory over the landowners for the first time.

In the meantime, the British elections of 1880 saw William Gladstone installed as prime minister, and his Land Act of 1881 was responsible for further improvements in the conditions of the tenant farmers. In the late spring of 1882, Lord Frederick Cavendish, chief secretary for Ireland, and T. H. Burke, the under-secretary (aides of the lord lieutenant, Britain's senior official in Ireland), were murdered in Dublin's Phoenix Park by members of an organization known as "the Invincibles." Though the Phoenix Park murders naturally outraged public opinion in Britain with respect to the Irish question, Parnell continued to work to obtain Home Rule as a form of, albeit limited, independence for his country, and continued to find a remarkable ally in Gladstone. However, Parnell was then caught up in a personal scandal. It became public knowledge that for the preceding ten years he had been having an affair with the wife of a fellow party member. He refused to resign, and the ensuing controversy caused a deep split in the party. Parnell fell ill, worsened rapidly, and died just a few months later at the age of forty-five.

38 TOP Lord Charles Beresford, F. E. Smith, Sir Edward Carson, and other Unionist leaders and protesters marching through the streets of Belfast on Ulster Day. They were heading for the town hall to sign a petition against Home Rule.

38 BOTTOM The Irish Volunteers, defenders of Home Rule, were led by the academic Eoin MacNeill.

39 On September 28, 1912, Ulster Unionist Party members signed a covenant blocking approval of Home Rule. Almost 500,000 citizens of Northern Ireland approved the signed document whereby Ulster swore loyalty to the United Kingdom.

REACTIONS TO HOME RULE

Not all Irishmen shared Parnell's beliefs about independence. For many Protestants, in fact, the concept of Home Rule corresponded more specifically to the idea of "Rome rule" and Catholic domination. Aware of the fact that it was only a matter of time before Home Rule was again on the political agenda, the Ulster Unionists, a party founded in 1885, decided to do something concrete to prevent it. Under the leadership of Sir Edward Carson, a Protestant lawyer from Dublin, they united as the Ulster Volunteer Force (UVF), with the precise intent of acting should Home Rule become law. Carson recognized that in order to be economically self-sufficient, the country required the heavy industry of Belfast. He was therefore convinced that the best way of suffocating the demands for Home Rule would be to partition the north from the rest of Ireland. In response to the growing power of the

UVF and to defend Home Rule throughout the country, the Irish Volunteers were assembled in the south of Ireland under the leadership of Eoin MacNeill.

In Britain the new government appeared to be favorable to the broader Irish demand for independence. The prime minister, Herbert Asquith, called for a parliamentary debate on the question of Home Rule for Ireland, in return for which he asked for the backing of the Irish Nationalist Party's members of Parliament.

Approved by the British parliament in 1912, the Home Rule Act was due to come into effect at the end of the First World War. During the conflict, many Irish nationalists fought alongside the British troops, convinced that this was the best way of swaying public opinion in Britain. However, a significant number of their compatriots remained skeptical.

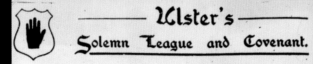

40-41 In the 1916 Easter Rising, running battles between soldiers and civilians devastated the streets of Dublin.

41 LEFT During the Rising, by virtue of their numerical superiority, the British troops wore down the rebels.

41 RIGHT Once the Rising had been suppressed and the fighting was over, the city streets displayed all too evident signs of the violence.

On Easter Monday, 1916, two small groups marched on Dublin: the Irish Volunteers, led by Patrick Pearse, and the Irish Citizens' Army, commanded by James Connolly. Taking the British forces, the Irish army, and the Dubliners themselves by surprise, the two groups managed to take possession of a number of strongholds in the city. The leaders established their headquarters in the general post office on O'Connell Street, from the steps of which Patrick Pearse read the following:

"Proclamation of the Provisional Government of the Republic of Ireland to the Irish People:

"Ireland, through us, summons her children to her flag and strikes for her freedom.

"The Irish Republic is entitled to, and hereby claims, the allegiance of every Irishman and Irish woman. The Republic guarantees religious and civil liberty, equal rights and equal opportunities of all its citizens, and declares its resolve to pursue the happiness and prosperity of the whole nation and of all its parts, cherishing all the children of the nation equally, and oblivious of the differences carefully fostered by an alien government, which have divided a minority in the past."

A few days later, however, unable to resist British military superiority, the rebels were vanquished. Of the insurgents, seventy-seven were condemned to death, although only fifteen were actually executed. Those who were executed included the leaders of the uprising: Pearse was hanged three days after the defeat of the uprising, and Connolly, the last to die, nine days after that defeat.

SOLDIERS ARE WE
OSE LIVES ARE PLEDGE To

REMEM
THOS
CLARE'S H

42 BOTTOM As well as being a soldier, Michael Collins was a leading political figure in the history of the Irish Free State.

43 LEFT Michael Collins, Arthur Griffith, and Eamon de Valera were among the members of Sinn Fein elected during the general election held in December 1919.

43 RIGHT AND BOTTOM To quell the conflict that broke out in 1921, the Royal Irish Constabulary called on the support of the Black and Tans, British soldiers whose nickname derived from their unusual uniforms and who were infamous for the violence with which they treated the rebels.

THE WAR WITH BRITAIN

Ireland's oldest Republican political party was founded in 1905. Following the Easter Rising of 1916, the Irish Republican Brotherhood evolved into the IRA — the Irish Republican Army. Its political wing, Sinn Féin (the name means "We Ourselves") put itself forward as the defender of absolute Irish independence, and achieved a runaway victory in the 1918 general election. The new members of Parliament refused to take their seats at Westminster and instead formed the Irish Assembly at the Mansion House in Dublin. Under the guidance of Eamon de Valera (the sole surviving leader from the 1916 Easter Rising), the party declared (but could not establish) Ireland's independence. The same period saw the emergence of Michael Collins, a new and charismatic leader committed to the struggle for Irish independence. A talented military organizer and the finance minister in the new government, Collins played a leading role for the IRA in the war with Britain that was soon to break out.

The pretext was offered by an episode in 1919 when two members of the Royal Irish Constabulary (RIC), the most authoritative instrument of British power in Ireland, were killed in County Tipperary. This marked the beginning of bloody battles that continued through to mid-1921. During the fighting the Royal Irish Constabulary, effectively the means whereby Great Britain exercised control over Ireland, were backed by the Black and Tans, British troops nicknamed thus because of their two-tone uniforms. The war became increasingly bloody and cruel, with the Black and Tans' violence doing nothing but fanning the flames of Irish hatred and hardening the resolve of the independence faction. For its part, the IRA organized itself into "flying squads," small groups of armed volunteers who prepared ambushes to entrap British troops. They enjoyed considerable success as they could move easily over terrain they knew intimately and could count on the support of the local people. A cease-fire was finally negotiated in 1921.

On December 6, 1921, the Anglo-Irish Treaty was signed in London. The agreement offered Ireland near-independence, with dominion status within the British Empire as the Irish Free State. However, it also offered the six predominantly Protestant counties of Derry, Antrim, Armagh, Fermanagh, Down, and Tyrone, all within the province of Ulster (Northern Ireland), the option of maintaining the preexisting political arrangements. Under the terms of the treaty, members of the Irish parliament would have continued to swear loyalty to the British Crown; thus the twenty-six southern counties would not be truly free but would be only nominally independent as the Irish Free State.

Negotiations continued at the treaty table for a number of months, with Arthur Griffith and Michael Collins representing Ireland. Under pressure from Lloyd George, they signed the agreement. Collins was convinced on the one hand that swearing loyalty to the British monarchy had only a symbolic value, and on the other that the Free State would soon absorb Northern Ireland. In reality, he was also well aware of the risk he was running, and actually said, "I

have signed my own death warrant." In his heart of hearts he knew that the members of the Irish parliament would not willingly accept subjection to the British Crown nor would they accept without a fight any move by Northern Ireland to reject inclusion in the Irish Free State. As was predictable, de Valera, who in the meantime had become the president of the newly declared Irish Free State, was furious with Collins for having signed the treaty with the British without his approval.

Civil war then ensued. Paradoxically, it was fought by the very men who just a year earlier had fought side by side for Ireland's independence, but who now opted for either the Free Staters, supporting the treaty signed in London, or the Republicans, who opposed it. Michael Collins was killed in a road ambush during the conflict in which de Valera and his companions were finally defeated in May 1923.

From this point on, the histories of the Irish Free State and Northern Ireland ran on parallel tracks; it is thus appropriate to treat them separately.

45 LEFT The 1921 Anglo-Irish Treaty concerned the division of Ireland and the creation of the Irish Free State in the south.

45 RIGHT Arthur Griffith and Michael Collins were members of the delegation that traveled to London to sign the treaty.

46 IN JULY 1922 CIVIL WAR BROKE OUT IN DUBLIN BETWEEN REPUBLICANS AND SUPPORTERS OF THE IRISH FREE STATE.

46-47 IRONICALLY, THE CIVIL WAR WAS FOUGHT BETWEEN MEN WHO JUST A YEAR EARLIER HAD STRUGGLED SIDE BY SIDE FOR THE INDEPENDENCE OF IRELAND.

Eamon de Valera gave the name Fianna Fáil ("Soldiers of Destiny") to the new political party he founded in 1926. After winning the general election of 1932, the party governed the Irish Free State uninterruptedly for sixteen years. A new constitution was introduced in 1938 that declared the absolute legislative independence of Ireland: Britain effectively renounced its right to exercise authority over the island. Renamed Éire, the Free State was to be governed by an Irish bicameral parliament, a president, and a prime minister.

In 1949, the present Republic of Ireland was declared and was officially constituted as a sovereign state; as such, it withdrew from the British Commonwealth. It then took Ireland twenty years to recover from the deep economic crisis into which it had plunged. Many of the young people, on whom the state was pinning its hopes of economic development and prosperity, were migrating to Britain in the quest for greater opportunity in a more prosperous economy. The situation improved after 1950, under a government led by Seán Lemass. Thanks to an expansionist policy, Lemass managed to curb the process of emigration, and during his government's administration, a large number of foreign companies began to invest in Ireland. Unemployment levels soon fell by a third.

The first people to benefit from this upturn in the Irish economy were the agricultural workers, who accounted for 20 percent of the total population.

48 LEFT AND RIGHT January 30, 1972, Londonderry, Northern Ireland: 13 unarmed protesters were brutally killed and another 13 were injured by British troops during the infamous Bloody Sunday massacre.

48-49 The funeral procession for the victims of the Bloody Sunday massacre departed from St. Mary's Church in Londonderry.

In 1955 Ireland became a member of the United Nations, and, on January 22, 1972, she became a full member of the European Economic Community. This led to a period of relative economic prosperity, although political stability proved harder to achieve. On January 30, 1972 (just eight days after joining the EEC), the country was rocked by the infamous Bloody Sunday events in Londonderry, Northern Ireland. On that day, thirteen unarmed citizens demonstrating for equal rights were killed by British troops of the Parachute Regiment. On February 2, a furious Irish crowd destroyed the British Embassy in Dublin. During the 1980s, Ireland suffered severely from the international economic recession, registering increases in unemployment and recording new waves of emigration.

An astute and flexible leader of the Fianna Fáil party, Charles Haughey won the general election of 1987 and took office as prime minister. In 1992, bombarded with continual accusations of poor financial administration and corruption, Haughey was obliged to tender his resignation and was replaced as prime minister by Albert Reynolds. Less than three years later, however, moral questions also led to Reynolds' downfall. The years in which he was a protagonist on the political scene were, in fact, blighted by scandals and saw the Catholic Church wielding considerable influence over numerous political and social questions. A succession of coalitions has since governed from 1994 to the present administration, led by the Fianna Fáil Party under a new leader, Bertie Ahern. Earlier, in 1990, Mary Robinson, an independent candidate backed by the Labour Party, was elected president of the Irish Republic. Her presence reinvigorated Irish politics as she reintroduced the values of integrity and liberalism. In 1997, another woman, Mary McAleese, a nationalist and committed Catholic, succeeded Mary Robinson as president. While considering the events that have marked Ireland's progress in the 1990s, mention has to be made of the flourishing economic development that has earned the country the nickname "the Celtic Tiger," with clear allusions to the strongly expanding economies of southeast Asia.

50 LEFT Belfast and Londonderry were the cities hardest hit by the conflict between Catholics and Protestants.

50 RIGHT Belfast, November 17, 1971: Suspecting the presence of a bomb, British troops blow up a car.

51 TOP British soldiers take up positions on Falls Road, Belfast. During the trouble that broke out November 17, 1971, five Catholics were killed and 60 were injured, and hundreds of houses were damaged.

51 BOTTOM Young Irish Catholics pelting the Royal Ulster Constabulary with stones in the Falls Road area.

On June 22, 1921, with the opening of a parliament located in the Belfast City Hall, Derry, Antrim, Fermanagh, Down, Tyrone, and Armagh (the six predominantly Protestant counties constituting the province of Ulster) became formally named Northern Ireland and recognized as a new geopolitical entity. Northern Ireland retained its ties to the British Crown, while to the south, the twenty-six predominantly Catholic counties of the largely self-governing Irish Free State as far as possible had rejected theirs. In order to understand the motives for the current situation in Northern Ireland, it is necessary to analyze the facts that led up to its creation. The north experienced a wave of colonization in the seventeenth century, and the Protestant descendants of the colonists tended to live alongside rather than to integrate with the Catholic population. The Protestants became the dominant economic group, and consequently industrial development in the north was inevitably associated with British commercial power. The British parliament at Westminster for its part ensured that the dominant

ly low-key approach, but when it did intervene, it never did so on behalf of the Catholics. The marches and the RUC's attitude contributed to the growing tension between the Catholic community and the Protestants, leading on occasion to the British Army's intervention. In these cases, however, restrictive measures imposed on the Catholics were always more severe than those imposed on the Protestants. The Irish Republican Army thus took up the defense of the Catholic people. Reorganized, it once again began to carry out a series of bombings and shootings throughout the North. "The Troubles," as the disorders in Ulster were called, were to blight Northern Ireland and Great Britain for almost thirty years, resulting in Britain's suspension in March 1972 of almost fifty-one years of semiautonomous rule by the Ulster government. In 1973, a conference held at Sunningdale, England, brought together representatives of the British and Northern Ireland governments and from the two sides of the political and religious divide. The major outcome was the creation of the Northern Ire-

land Executive, involving both Unionists and Nationalists, with the aim of more equitable rule in Ulster. However, in May 1974, the predominantly Catholic Ulster Workers' Council organized a general strike, while the strongly Protestant Ulster Defence Association (UDA) blocked roads. These disruptions paralyzed the power stations and other services. In the same week, the UDA detonated four car bombs in Dublin, killing thirty-three people. With the

political class was pro-British, while the Unionists (the political party that favored close ties with Britain) guaranteed that Protestant control was maintained, even in areas with a Catholic majority. This was the case, for example, in Derry, a city that was two-thirds Catholic but which, through control and manipulation, elected a council that was two-thirds Protestant. This situation, which saw the Catholics discriminated against by the Protestants, endured for decades. "Equal rights for all" was the demand made by the Northern Ireland Civil Rights Association, founded in 1967. The Catholic community gave the association significant support and participated in many protest marches. During these events, the strongly Protestant police force (the Royal Ulster Constabulary, or RUC) took a general-

intention of destabilizing the government, the IRA carried out a series of terrorist attacks in Great Britain. A pub bombing in Birmingham in 1974 killed twenty-one people, and another seven were killed in simultaneous attacks in Woolwich and Guildford. To respond to this, Britain introduced the Prevention of Terrorism Act; it permitted preventive incarceration for long periods without precise charges. On the basis of this act, four innocent people were arrested for the Guildford bombings and received jail sentences of fifteen years. Their story, which attracted public sympathy and indignation, inspired Jim Sheridan's famous film, *In the Name of the Father.* Six Irishmen were sentenced to life imprisonment for the Birmingham attack, but those sentences were revoked in 1991.

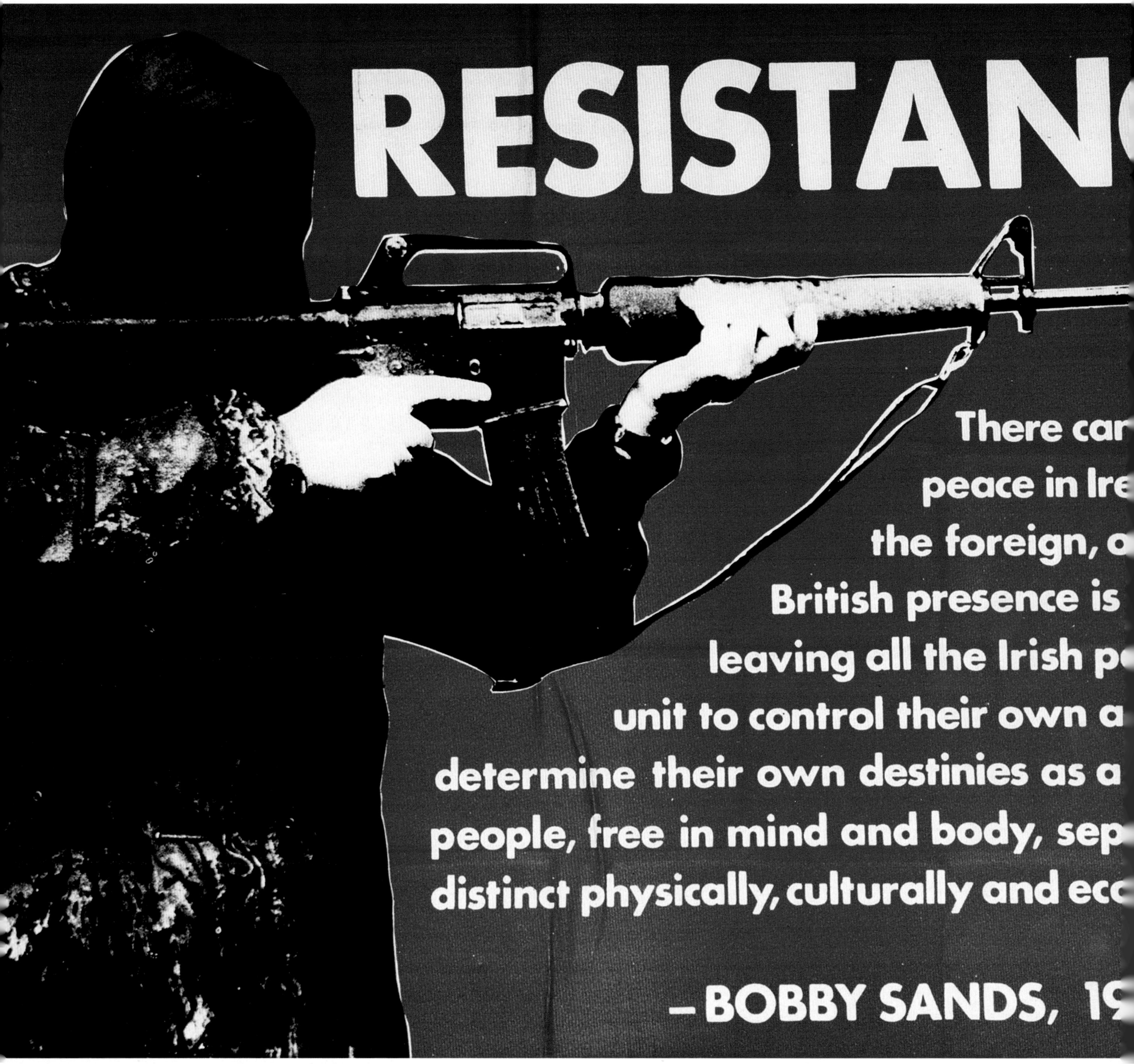

RESISTANC

There car
peace in Ire
the foreign, o
British presence is
leaving all the Irish pe
unit to control their own a
determine their own destinies as a
people, free in mind and body, sep
distinct physically, culturally and ec

– BOBBY SANDS, 19

53 LEFT BELFAST: ARMED BRITISH SOLDIERS ATTEMPT TO SUBDUE THE WAVE OF VIOLENCE THAT BROKE OUT FOLLOWING THE DEATH OF BOBBY SANDS.

53 RIGHT A HUGE CROWD, AS WELL AS MANY IRA MEMBERS, ATTENDED THE FUNERAL OF BOBBY SANDS.

53 BOTTOM IN 1981, FURTHER TROUBLES FOLLOWED THE KILLING OF TWO YOUNG IRISHMEN BY BRITISH TROOPS.

While the violence began to diminish in the 1980s, a solution to the Irish political and sectarian problems appeared to be no closer. The situation was aggravated by the birth of new parties, groups, and secessionist wings, each with its own agenda. The IRA, for example, split into two factions, one official and one extremist. The Protestants for their part formed Loyalist paramilitary groups. In an attempt to find a solution to the crisis, the Anglo-Irish Agreement of 1986 promoted and formalized cooperation between Britain and the Republic of Ireland. Subsequently, Albert Reynolds and John Major, the Irish and British prime ministers, signed the Downing Street Declaration in an attempt to resolve the delicate question of Northern Ireland.

On August 31, 1994, twenty-five years after the beginning of the Troubles, Gerry Adams, the Sinn Féin leader, unexpectedly announced on behalf of the IRA the "complete cessation of military operations." Two months later, Ulster's paramilitary Loyalists decided to follow suit. In February 1995, after fresh negotiations, the British and Irish governments drew up two documents in an attempt to satisfy some of the Republicans' constitutional demands. However,

the negotiations ran into further difficulties and only resumed after the intervention of an international commission. Its president was American senator George Mitchell, who set six conditions for continuation of negotiations (the so-called Mitchell Principles). The hopes for lasting peace proved to be in vain; on February 9, 1996, a bomb exploded in London near Canary Wharf, killing two people and injuring many more. After various vicissitudes, negotiations recommenced in September 1997. On April 10, 1998, the historic Good Friday Agreement was signed, a highly important event in Northern Ireland's history. John Hume, representing the Social Democratic and Labour Party, favored Ulster's reunification with the Republic of Ireland; David Trimble, representing the Unionist Parties, favored retention of ties with Great Britain. The two leaders committed themselves to respecting the principles of "partnership, equality, and mutual respect as the basis of relationships within Northern Ireland" and to using "exclusively democratic and peaceful means of resolving differences on political issues." The path to true peace is still long, but now at least the foundations have been laid.

A LOOK AT LITERATURE

A country extraordinarily rich in novelists, poets, and playwrights, Ireland boasts a literary tradition that blossomed at the end of the seventeenth century and continues to produce exceptional authors. No fewer than four winners of the Nobel Prize for Literature have been born in Ireland. Rebel spirits and frequently the spokesmen for political ideologies, Irish authors have associated their lives and literary activities with Ireland's destiny. Irish politics, religion, landscapes, and social conditions were the raw materials mined by the famous and not-so-famous men and women who have made such significant contributions to the nation's culture. Irish literary tradition developed within a very delicate sociopolitical context. It should be remembered that between 1690 and 1720, the period in which the Penal Laws were enforced, Catholics were denied rights of property, education, religious freedom, and political participation. They were also increasingly driven into poverty, often because of the deficiencies of British governance. It is understandable that the Irish people felt the need to denounce these injustices. John Toland (1620–1720), author of numerous caustic pamphlets, provided one of the first and most important testimonies. His polemical book, *Christianity Not Mysterious,* was publicly burned in Dublin. Another satirical writer worthy of note is Laurence Sterne (1713–1768), author of *The Life and Opinions of Tristram Shandy,* a work in which Sterne experimented with a new style of writing that flew in the face of the literary conventions. For example, he faced a blank white page with one printed black and dedicated a whole chapter to a single sentence. However, the undisputed master, the greatest writer of his era and one of the greatest satirical authors of all time was Jonathan Swift (1667–1745), the author of no fewer than seventy-five satirical pamphlets

highlighting the widespread hypocrisy, corruption, and immorality of eighteenth-century Dublin. His most famous and popular work, *Gulliver's Travels,* was published in 1726; it is a stinging attack on the society of his era. Among the late eighteenth-century authors, mention must be made of Oliver Goldsmith (1730–1774), author of the romantic novel *The Vicar of Wakefield,* and Richard Brinsley Sheridan (1751–1816), responsible for sophisticated comedies such as *The School for Scandal.* Toward the end of the nineteenth century, while attempts were being made to establish Home Rule for Ireland, the country witnessed a renaissance in art, culture, and the Irish identity. In 1893, men of letters such as Douglas Hyde and Eoin MacNeill founded the Gaelic League, which emphasized the wealth of the Gaelic language and promoted the teaching of the Irish language in schools. Other writers involved in the diffusion of Anglo-Irish literature included Lady Gregory, John Millington Synge, and George Russell. They were interested in the ancient Celtic stories associated with the legendary figure of Cúchulainn, and through their works they contributed to the creation of the image of a mythical Ireland stirred by warriors and epic battles. The name that leaps off any page listing Irish literary greats is, of course, that of William Butler Yeats (1865–1939), an aristocratic Protestant and a defender of Irish liberty and independence, yet also personally committed to the promotion of a national literature in English. The winner of the Nobel Prize for Literature in 1923, Yeats was also a poet, and playwright and one of the founders of the Irish National Theatre. Fairies, elves, and leprechauns appear in his collections of folk stories *(Fairy and Folk Tales of the Irish Peasantry* and *Fairy and Folk Tales),* evidence of his deep interest in Celtic folklore.

Seamus Heaney (1939–), who in 1995 won the Nobel Prize, is widely regarded as the "most important English-speaking poet since Yeats" and represents his ideal heir. *Death of a Naturalist* is one of Heaney's early anthologies, while the later *Wintering Out* and *North* are the fruit of profound political reflection.

Sean O'Casey (1880–1964), a playwright and contemporary of Yeats, was also involved with the Abbey Theatre. Born and bred in the poorer quarters of Dublin, his works describe with stark realism the poverty of the city's lower class. Another of the Irish winners of the Nobel Prize is George Bernard Shaw (1856–1950), a playwright, narrator, and essayist born in Dublin and marked by a difficult childhood. Plays were the means by which the author decided to denounce and recount his personal dramas as well as social ills such as prostitution *(Mrs. Warren's Profession).* His masterpiece is *Saint Joan,* a tragicomic account of the destiny that man reserves for saviors, saints, and heroines. An exceptional master of theatrical technique, Shaw was awarded the Nobel Prize in 1925, perhaps the ultimate recognition for a "preacher dressed as a juggler," as he described himself.

Bram Stoker (1847–1912), a writer and theater critic born in Dublin and the author of a number of novels and novellas, occupies a special place on the nineteenth-century literary scene. His name is inevitably associated with the unorthodox enterprises of Count Dracula, the world's most famous vampire, still active in his calling if only in any number of films, cartoons, and comic books. The second half of the nineteenth century also witnessed the literary debut of Oscar Wilde (1856–1900), born and bred in the more salubrious areas of Dublin and a habitué of the London and Paris salons where he became the object of various scandals, censures, and condemnations. An eccentric nonconformist, Wilde has left us with a series of sharp social satires *(Lady Windermere's Fan, An Ideal Husband, The Importance of Being Earnest)*, essays, poems, theatrical works *(Salomé),* and a novel, *The Picture of Dorian Gray,* that have become an emblem of aestheticism in art.

In the meantime, one of the undisputed masters of modern literature was emerging in Dublin: James Joyce (1882–1941), an author rightly credited with having developed styles and idioms that revolutionized the literature of the early twentieth century. After making his debut as a poet, Joyce consolidated his reputation with narrative works such as *Dubliners,* in which he denounced the paralysis he believed to be afflicting public life in Dublin, the city of his birth. This was one of the reasons the author decided to spend most of his life abroad. Following the publication of *A Portrait of the Artist as a Young Man,* which introduced the character Stephen Daedalus, Joyce presented his most famous work, *Ulysses,* a dazzling, extraordinarily introspective novel in which the confines of language are stretched in every direction. The book recounts a day in the life of Leopold Bloom, an Irish Jew.

The writer and dramatist Samuel Beckett (1906–1989), a close friend of Joyce until the latter's death, is another of the protagonists of modern Irish literature, and was awarded the Nobel Prize in 1969. Despite being known as a "man of few words," Beckett was actually a very prolific writer and published novels such as *Molloy, Malone Dies,* and *The Unnamable* and plays such as *Waiting for Godot.*

THE GREEN AND THE SEA

58 **CLOCKWISE FROM LEFT** Pastures in County Antrim. The cliffs of Clonakilty Bay in County Cork. On the way to the Gap of Dunloe in County Kerry by horse-drawn carriage. The bogs of County Mayo.

59 Donegal offers a sequence of peninsulas, promontories, and mountains.

60 Crops, pastureland, and ruined towers punctuate the green landscape of County Cork.

61 **TOP LEFT** Newgrange in County Meath is a passage tomb built in about 3000 b.c., a period in which man had yet to begin using metals.

61 **TOP RIGHT** Kylemore Abbey, one of the pearls lying in the heart of Connemara.

61 **BOTTOM** The Shannon, Ireland's greatest river, flows into the Atlantic Ocean, forming an estuary more than ten miles long.

THE GREEN AND THE SEA

Washed by the Atlantic Ocean and separated from Great Britain by the Irish Sea, the Emerald Isle is situated to the far northwest of Europe, the last green outpost of the Old Continent. From an administrative point of view, the country is divided into thirty-two counties: twenty-six in the Irish Republic and six in Northern Ireland. The island is also traditionally divided into four provinces: Leinster, Munster, Connaught, and Ulster.

Commencing in the province of Leinster, situated in the center and southeast of the island, the visitor initially encounters the counties of Wexford, Carlow, and Kilkenny. This is the sunniest and the driest area of the country, delimited inland by three rivers, the Nore, Barrow, and Slaney and by the remote Blackstairs Mountains, which represent a geographical confine between County Wexford and County Carlow. Running through verdant pastures and wooded valleys, past Christian ruins from the medieval period and small villages, the Nore and Barrow flow down from the beautiful hills and valleys to the north of New Ross. Along County Wexford's entire coast stretch spectacular sandy beaches, while farther south the coastline provides ideal bird-watching territory. This is the area comprising the Wexford Slobs, the lakes of Lady's Island and Tacumshane, the Saltee Islands off Kilmore Quay, and the Hook Head Peninsula.

To the north, County Wicklow offers some of Ireland's wildest and most stunning mountain landscapes. It is also the location of the Paleo-Celtic monastery of Glendalough, once known throughout Europe as an important center of learning. The bordering County Kildare presents a patchwork of cultivated farmland. The region is dominated by the vast Curragh plain that, with a large racecourse and a dozen stables, is the heartland of Irish horse racing. To the west are the counties of Laois and Offaly, a tranquil region off the beaten tourist trail, while a little farther north are the counties of Meath, Louth, Westmeath, and Longford, presenting the archetypal green and rural image of Ireland. County Louth, the smallest of the Republic's twenty-six counties, lies on a stretch of coast featuring two sizeable towns, Drogheda and Dundalk. The undulating hinterland rises to the northeast in a mountainous area of rare beauty: the Cooley Peninsula, a place in which reality merges into the legends of Táin Bó Cuailnge (the Cattle Raid of Cooley), one of the best known epics of Irish literature. Apart from a number of strikingly beautiful beaches, this part of Ireland is also famed for its inland areas and the lush, fertile farmlands through which the River Boyne and its tributaries flow. The river gave its name to the Battle of the Boyne fought July 1, 1690, seven km (four and a half miles) from Drogheda, when the troops of King William III, upholder of the Protestant cause, fought and won against those of the deposed Catholic king, James II. County Meath boasts the island's most fascinating historical sites, dating back as far as the Stone Age and offering over forty prehistoric monuments within the Brugh na Boinne complex at Navan.

The county is also worthy of note for the celebrated Kells Monastery founded by St. Columba in the sixth century. It later became the principal Columban monastery in Ireland after the monks compiling the celebrated illuminated manuscript known as the *Book of Kells* sought refuge there in 807 as they fled from Viking invaders. The town of Trim boasts the ruins of the largest Anglo-Norman castle in Ireland; in 1995, it was used as a set for a number of scenes in the film *Braveheart,* starring Mel Gibson.

Neighboring County Westmeath's major attraction is its numerous lakes, Lough Sheelin, Lough Lene, Lough Derravaragh, Lough Owel, and Lough Ennell among them. Also worthy of mention is the picturesque village of Castlepollard, the ideal point of departure for a visit to Tullynally Castle, one of the country's most attractive and romantic fortifications. Farther to the

north, County Monaghan is punctuated by rounded hills formed from glacial detritus, while the area around the county town of Cavan is known for its myriad small lakes.

The center and southwest of Ireland lie within the province of Munster. Verdant undulating hills roll through County Waterford to the coast in the far south, with its dramatic cliffs punctuated by broad bays and isolated beaches. On the border with County Tipperary, the austere Rock of Cashel rises on a hill in the heart of the Golden Vale. This imposing medieval stronghold was long the seat of the ancient kings of Munster and was subsequently donated to the church. The spectacular architectural complex is composed of the ruins of an ancient castle, a cathedral, and a Romanesque chapel, and is surrounded by a curtain wall. The Golden Vale, one of southern Ireland's most fertile regions, is a vast expanse of culti-

vated land surrounded by mountain ranges; the Galty Mountains and the Glen of Aherlow are particularly attractive. Less than a kilometer farther to the west, set in gently sloping expanse of green fields, stands what remains of Hore Abbey, founded by the Cistercian monks in 1265. In neighboring County Limerick with its numerous medieval castles and towers, Castle Matrix, a perfectly preserved fifteenth-century tower house containing a wealth of precious objets d'art, is well worth visiting.

Farther north, in County Clare, stands Bunratty Castle, one of the finest examples of medieval Irish castle architecture, where visitors can still experience the magic of the past. Along the southern edge of the county to Loop Head stretches kilometer after kilometer of dramatic coastline, with the spectacular Cliffs of Moher (224 m/ 800 ft. high) falling sheer to the sea farther north. The landscape changes around the largest town in County Clare, Ennis, which is surrounded by low-lying cultivated lands. The scenery here provides a complete contrast with the uplands of the Burren in the far northwest of the county, a massive limestone and clay plateau. The name of the town derives from ancient word *boireann,* which in Burren means "rocky land." This region has nothing in common with the traditional image of the Emerald Isle, but gives the impression of being part of a different world. It is a gray, harsh, and barren land, with strong contrasts deriving from an unusual combination of rock, light, and water. There are some 30,000 hectares (74,000 acres) of land at an altitude of 300 meters (990 ft.) that extend for 160 km (100 miles) with dolmens, subterranean grottoes, tiny watercourses that disappear into the ground, and turloughs (small lakes that dry up during the summer).

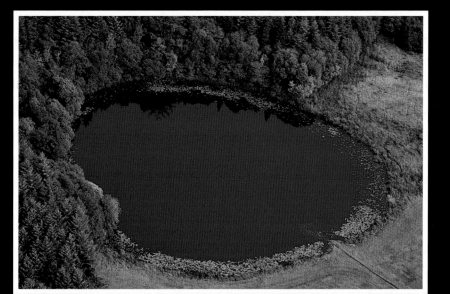

64-65 A CHARACTERISTIC HORSE-CARRIAGE ("JAUNTING CAR") BOWLING ALONG THE NARROW LANES OF KILLARNEY NATIONAL PARK NEAR MUCKROSS HOUSE, A MAGNIFICENT
VICTORIAN HOME AND ONE OF THE MOST IMPORTANT HOUSES OF HISTORIC AND ARTISTIC INTEREST IN IRELAND.

65 LEFT The Skellig Islands, gigantic limestone outcrops, are situated 7.5 miles off the coast of County Kerry.

65 RIGHT Sligo Bay is an extensive inlet enclosed by high, rocky cliffs, within which is situated the town of Sligo.

The counties of Cork (the largest in Ireland) and Kerry, with its incredible landscapes, complete the province.

The gentle countryside of County Cork transforms toward the west, along a coastline laced with bays and hidden inlets, into the dramatic panorama offered by the wild peninsulas of the extreme southwest; Mizen Head, Sherkin Island, and bird-thronged Clear Island are all truly spectacular. Situated at the mouth of the River Bandon, Kinsale is the best-known seaside town on the southwest coast, frequented above all by lovers of sailing and deep-sea fishing. County Kerry offers magical landscapes composed of mountains, hills, lakes, and the sea. Three easily recognizable areas, each with distinct characteristics, call out for exploration. They are the Dingle Peninsula, where the ruins of numerous ancient monasteries help create a mystical atmosphere; the Iveragh Peninsula, circumscribed by the Ring of Kerry (a famous panoramic road about 180 km/110 miles long, which also includes Killarney with its extensive national park; and the Kenmare River, framed by the Iveragh and Beara Peninsulas (the second actually forming part of County Cork).

The Oyster County, as Galway is known, is one of the largest counties making up Connaught, Ireland's westernmost province. Divided into two by Lough Corrib, the county is distinctly different on either shore. To the east extends a fertile area that has been cultivated for centuries, while to the west instead opens the wild reaches of Connemara, characterized by great marshes, picturesque mountains, and beaches of white sand. Farther along the coast is County Mayo, considered to be the most wild and traditional region of the country. Often called Ireland's equivalent to the Far West, this is a remote and solitary area dominated to the north by extensive peat bogs. To the southwest, Westport on the shores of Clew Bay is worth visiting, while to

66 THIS PART OF THE COAST OF NORTH ANTRIM IS KNOWN AS THE GIANT'S CAUSEWAY, AFTER AN ANCIENT LEGEND INVOLVING A LOVE RIVALRY BETWEEN TWO GIANTS. SHOWN HERE IS THE STRETCH BETWEEN PORTBALLINTRAE AND PORTRUSH.

67 THE GREAT HEXAGONAL COLUMNS OF BASALT EMERGING FROM THE SEA ALONG THE GIANT'S CAUSEWAY RESULTED FROM THE CRYSTALLIZATION OF INCANDESCENT LAVA ERUPTING FROM A SUBTERRANEAN FISSURE AROUND 60 MILLION YEARS AGO.

THE GREEN AND THE SEA

the northwest lies the county town of Foxford, famous for its woolen mills. To the west of County Mayo lies the inland County Roscommon, a generally low-lying flat area largely composed of bogs and pastures. On the borders of the counties of Sligo and Leitrim rise the high, rugged Curlew Mountains. County Sligo boasts the beautiful Benbulben and Knochnarea Mountains, the pretty Loughs Gill and Glencar, and the widest range of imposing menhirs and other megalithic monuments in

the whole of Ireland. Among the most interesting sites are the Neolithic cemetery of Carrowmore located to the west of Sligo itself and the prehistoric village of Carrowkeel situated on the peaks of the Bricklieve Mountains.

Adjoining Sligo is County Leitrim, bisected north to south by Lough Allen. Long narrow valleys and high mountains characterize the landscape. The southern part is dominated by the course of the River Shannon and drumlins (characteristic rounded hills). County Donegal, in the northwest corner of the island and second in extent only to County Cork, offers the

greatest variety of landscapes in Ireland. Serried promontories and peninsulas characterize the coastline, while the inland areas feature alternating valleys, rivers, and peat hills.

The northeastern part of Ireland is home to the six counties of Ulster. Arriving from the southeast, the first are County Armagh and County Down, which share a common heritage as sites associated with the story of St. Patrick. Farther north runs the coastline of the counties of Antrim and Londonderry, among the most scenic in Ireland. In particular, the northwest tip of Antrim features the beautiful Nine Glens of Antrim, green fingers of land ending in spectacular cliffs. Even more stunning is the nearby Giant's Causeway, an extraordinary geological phenomenon created 60 million years ago by lava produced in a subterranean volcanic explosion. Once solidified, the lava formed layers of dense basalt that subsequently cracked into regular polygonal blocks. County Derry, by contrast, offers a more reassuring landscape of fertile cultivated lands dotted with tiny villages extending toward the beautiful Sperrin Mountains on the northern border of County Tyrone. Wild and deserted, the mountains rise to altitudes of up to 750 meters (2,475 ft.). Lastly, gentle County Fermanagh attracts many visitors, particularly to Lough Erne, an extensive range of lakes and islands in a pleasant and fertile rural setting.

68 LEFT DINGLE PENINSULA IN COUNTY KERRY OFFERS SPECTACULAR VIEWS OF THE SEA AND MOUNTAINS.

68 RIGHT CELTIC CROSSES IN THE GRAVEYARD AT THE ROCK OF CASHEL IN THE TIPPERARY PLAIN.

68 BOTTOM LOUGH KINALE IN WESTMEATH OFFERS ATTRACTIVE VIEWS ALONG ITS SHORES AS WELL AS ABUNDANT FISH, A REAL ATTRACTION FOR ANGLERS.

69 ABANDONED FARMHOUSES SUFFOCATED BY CLIMBING PLANTS DOT THE FIELDS NEAR HEADFORD IN GALWAY.

THE SHAMROCK
ISLAND

It has a name of its own, "country green" — the color of the Irish countryside. A landscape distinguished and dominated from its northernmost to its southernmost tip by myriad shades of green. It's ever present from the wilds of Donegal to the fertile lowlands of Tipperary and the undulating pastures of the midland plains. This characteristic hue has earned Ireland the appropriate sobriquet of "the Green Island." Visitors can endlessly immerse themselves in verdant rolling or gently sloping expanses bathed in an almost surreal silence, broken perhaps only by the whispering breeze or the rustle of the waves breaking on a not too distant shore. When visitors begin to explore these areas, they gain the impression that some master artist of the past must have had great reward creating the incredible palette of different greens (according to some estimates, no fewer than forty shades) that gradually emerge as they proceed. Much of the Irish countryside is composed of a patchwork of fields given over to sheep grazing (or, to a lesser extent, cattle grazing). It should not be forgotten that the Irish economy is based principally upon the raising of these animals. There is also an ancient craft tradition associated with the weaving of wool to produce the famous Irish tweed.

A more detailed look at the principal agricultural regions of the country could well begin with the first large green area to the southwest of Dublin, the area that encompasses County Kildare's cultivated slopes, with their open fields and rough pastures. This is the Ireland of the Curragh, the vast plain of soft turf that has always provided the ideal terrain for horse racing. Farther to the west, without crossing the natural boundary of the River Shannon, the backbone of the country that winds for 372 km (230 miles) from the slopes of the Cuilcagh Mountains down to the Atlantic Ocean, visitors pass through the central counties, green and rural Ireland par excellence. These are the extensive Irish midlands, rightly considered as Ireland's "green lung." The region comprises, to the south, the counties of Laois and Offaly; to the west, those of Westmeath, Meath, Longford, and Louth; and to the north, those of Cavan and Monaghan. These are areas of lush pastures, dotted with lakes and bogs. County Offaly in particular, delimited to the east by the Bog of Allen and to the west by Boora Bog, is strewn throughout with bog land and marsh. But these areas have value far beyond their incomparable natural beauty. They conserve invaluable testimony to the past: Celtic crosses, Norman abbeys, and Gothic Revival castles, as well as the remains of ancient settlements. In the Boyne Valley, for example, County Meath, a fluvial area characterized by extremely fertile agricultural land, has numerous Neolithic mounds, portal tombs, and sacred enclosures that were colonized during the Stone Age. These archaeological treasures mark the cradle of Irish civilization. In the far northwest of the country, County Donegal offers other greens. Its inland regions are a sequence of rivers, valleys, and hills. Here the air is scented with peat and the rich turf is walled and hedged into a patchwork of emerald green meadows where Merino, South Down, Leicester, and Cheviot sheep graze contentedly.

70-71 The landscape of Donegal, like most of Ireland, is marked by the millenary toil of man.

72-73 Windows with frames flaked by the wind and rain reflect the countryside south of Malin, on the Inishowen Peninsula in Ireland's extreme north.

74 TOP Social life in Donegal's rural villages revolves around the pub. This is one of Ardara's most popular pubs.

74 BOTTOM Elegant Georgian streets and old townhouses characterize Rathmelton, on the Fanad Peninsula in northwest Ireland.

75 Ancient walls, ancient faces: This pub in Teelin in Donegal seems to encapsulate the Irish spirit.

76-77 A modern Intercity train crosses the flats of County Offaly in the heart of the island.

78-79 Road improvements are being made throughout Ireland, in this case in Westmeath.

NANCY'S CHAS M'HUGH NANCY'S

LICENSED TO SELL WINE SPIRITS, & BEER,
FOR CONSUMPTION ON OR OFF THE PREMISES. 7-DAY LICENCE.

GUINNESS
FOR STRENGTH

NANCYS

80 This long country road takes to the Gap of Dunloe. Tourists take a carriage or horse through it, rarely a car.

80-81 A tree-lined road runs past a country estate in late summer in County Tipperary, in south-central Ireland.

82-83 Fields of heather and grazing land in County Antrim, Northern Ireland.

84 The dream of every naturalist, Ireland has many practically unspoiled nature reserves. The water plants seen here inhabit the River Lee in Gearagh, an alluvial plain of marshes and woods that today is a paradise for ornithologists.

85 Like long, shiny strands of hair, these flowering river plants have colonized both banks of the Bandon River in County Cork.

86-87 Ferns, ivy, and mosses crowd this corner of paradise in Killarney National Park, County Kerry. Studded with ruined castles and abbeys, the park includes the Upper Lake, Muckross Lake, Lough Leane, and Long Range River.

88-89 Lough Gill in County Sligo has a magical atmosphere. A legend tells that the chimes of a silver bell buried in the lake bed can be heard, but only by those who have never sinned.

90-91 Bogland in the countryside of Bangor in County Mayo marks the boundary of Erris, a territory named after the barons who owned the land for centuries.

92-93 Flat-topped Benbulben surveys the Sligo countryside. W. B. Yeats, the great Irish poet who was born in these parts, was buried in a small cemetery at the foot of the mountain.

94-95 The hills around Lough Poolacappu in County Galway are bare and menacing despite their low height.

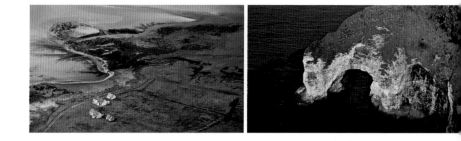

96 Flat fields abruptly become sloping scrub and rocky headland at Ballycotton Bay on the Celtic Sea. Historically, lack of land and poor soil drove many Irish to seek their fortune overseas.

97 TOP Views of Ireland's east coast: The green, the sand, and the rocks create landscapes of rare beauty.

97 BOTTOM Fanad Head in Donegal weathers the gales in the extreme north of Ireland.

WHERE

THE CURRAGHS REIGN

The green countryside and the many-toned sea: an indissoluble pairing. The sea, of course, simultaneously protects and torments Ireland, and the Irish are never more than 100 km (60 miles) or so from the coast, where the blue of the sky blends into the colors of the ocean. The history and life of the land and its inhabitants are intimately bound up with the sea; it's a tormented history filled with men who during periods of great hardship committed themselves to that sea as they set sail toward the New World. And still today the sea offers only an uncertain life for the many Irishmen who devote themselves to fishing and whose livelihoods and destinies are still dependent upon the unpredictable waters. The more than 3,000 km (1,860 miles) of Ireland's shoreline, punctuated by tongues of sand, bays, hidden inlets, cliffs, and islands, is home to the country's most spectacular scenery. On the most attractive western coast are fishing villages, beaches, and cliffs offering unforgettable panoramic vistas.

Magical, timeless places cloaked in mystery and legend where one breathes the heady scent of salt brought in on the sea breeze and where life appears to proceed at a slower, unhurried pace. County Cork, in the far south of the country, has the enchanting fishing village of Baltimore; from there ferries depart for tiny Sherkin Island and for steep and rocky Clear Island, one of the *gaeltacht* islands

where the ancient Irish language is still spoken, and also home of an ornithological observatory. Farther west along the coast lies Mizen Head Peninsula with its broad, sandy beaches and towering cliffs. Moving on up the coast and rounding Sheep's Head, the next landmarks to appear are Bantry Bay and the Beara Peninsula. Farther north, in the county of the same name, is the famous Ring of Kerry, a panoramic circular route winding for about 180 km (110 miles) through mountainous landscapes and stunning bays and cliffs. On a clear day the Skellig Islands can be seen from Bray Head, the extreme tip of Valentia Island. Isolated and mysterious, the Skelligs are two splinters of rock rising from the ocean about 13 km (8 miles) off the coast. Small Skellig is inhabited only by thousands of seabirds. In Great Skellig are the remains of an ancient monastery, St. Finian's Abbey, from which one can admire a beautiful panorama. Farther north extends the 160-kilometer (100-mile) coastline of the Dingle Peninsula, one of Ireland's most unspoiled regions and one in which the Celtic traditions are kept alive and the ancient Gaelic language is still spoken. It is an archaeologist's paradise, with some 2,000 sites dating from the Iron Age to the Middle Ages. The landscape is dreamlike, punctuated by cliffs sculpted by the ocean waves, and with endless stretches of sand and stone-built villages. These are the romantic locations that have inspired writers, poets, and directors such as the Englishman David Lean, who set the film *Ryan's Daughter* on the peninsula. Beyond the peninsula lie the uninhabited Blasket Islands, Europe's westernmost outpost. To the north, offering panoramas over the Atlantic are several kilometers of County Clare's fabulous cliffs. But there are also ocean-fronting villages and towns such as Kilkee, a bustling small resort with a magnificent beach that at its westernmost tip meets the towering cliffs of Duggerna Rocks. The panorama is completed by the Cliffs of Moher ("Cliffs of Ruin"), below whose sheer 200-meter (660-ft.) tops the open Atlantic Ocean rolls westward for 5,000 km (3,100 miles) until it washes the shores of the New World. From a distance the cliffs appear to be impregnable bulwarks. Composed of strata of clayey schist alternating with sandstone, the cliffs stretch for 8 km (5 miles) between the towns of Doolin and Liscannor; they constitute the ideal habitat for thousands of seabirds. It is worth visiting the cliff tops just to hear the deafening roar of the waves beating against the rocks and to gaze out to the Aran Islands (Inishmore, Inishmaan, and Inisheer) located just to the north. Limestone outcrops offering lunar landscapes, the islands are ranged in an oblique line across the entrance to Galway Bay, about 10 km (6 miles) from the mainland. Just up the coast is Connemara, one of Ireland's most unspoiled areas. "To Hell or to Connaught" was the famous phrase used in reference to Connemara, the area of County Galway to which Oliver Cromwell exiled those Irishmen whose lands he had confiscated under the 1652 Act of Settlement. In effect, given that 80 percent of the area is barren, it can hardly be called hospitable, but for those who decide to visit this solitary and still traditional corner of Ireland, the setting is anything but "infernal." The Connemara coastline with its bays and tiny windswept islands is extraordinarily beautiful. From Galway City, the coast road leads to the villages of Spiddal, Rossaveell, and Gortmore, the port at the entrance to magnificent Kilkieran Bay, dotted with large and small islands and penin-

sulas. There follows an area distinguished by small lakes and peat hills, the very rugged Bertraghboy Bay with its myriad small islands and finally Cashel Bay, an authentic paradise of nature and tranquillity. Farther on rises Slyne Head, beyond which there is only the ocean, rimmed by brilliant white beaches. Here, at the foot of Errisbeg Mountain (whose summit offers an unrivaled panorama) stands Roundstone, a village renowned for its lobster fishing. The coastline of remote County Mayo winds between Clew Bay and Killala Bay, alternating vast sandy beaches with menacing cliffs. Some 8 km (5 miles) from Clew Bay, also known as the "Bay of the Three Hundred and Sixty-Five Islands" after the countless outcrops scattered across it, is the town of Westport, which the Victorian architect James Wyatt enriched with broad, tree-lined streets. Just off the coast lies Achill Island, the country's largest island, now linked to the mainland by a bridge. The N15 coast road leaves Sligo and follows the southern part of Donegal Bay, a seemingly endless sequence of small resorts and long, sandy beaches and strands. The county's coastline winds for 300 km (185 miles) of promontories and peninsulas toward Europe's highest cliffs, Slieve League, and beyond to the famous valley of Glencolumbkille. This valley has been continuously inhabited from prehistoric times onward as confirmed by the tombs, dolmens, and early Christian Celtic crosses scattered throughout the area as far as Glen Bay. In the far north of the country, exploration of Ireland's western seaboard is completed by the incredible scenery of the Giant's Causeway, lying to the east in County Antrim. This natural phenomenon is composed of almost 40,000 basalt pillars so regular in shape that they appear sculpted by some master mason. So suggestive are they that myriad fantastic legends have arisen regarding their origins. One of these tall tales claims that the giant Fionn Mac Cumhaill created the causeway in order to reach the Scottish island of Staffa. This was the home of the woman he loved (or, according to others, that his warrior rival Finn Gall loved), so he built a road across the sea supported on stone pillars.

102-103 Sharp spurs of rock thrust out from Mizen Head, County Cork, into the turbulent Celtic Sea. The large rifts have been created by the power of the waves.

104-105 The steep cliffs that defy easy approach encourage seabirds to nest there despite the sheer drop. The strong uplift of the wind assists the flight of the heavier birds and allows them to glide without effort. They can even hang in the same spot for minutes at a time.

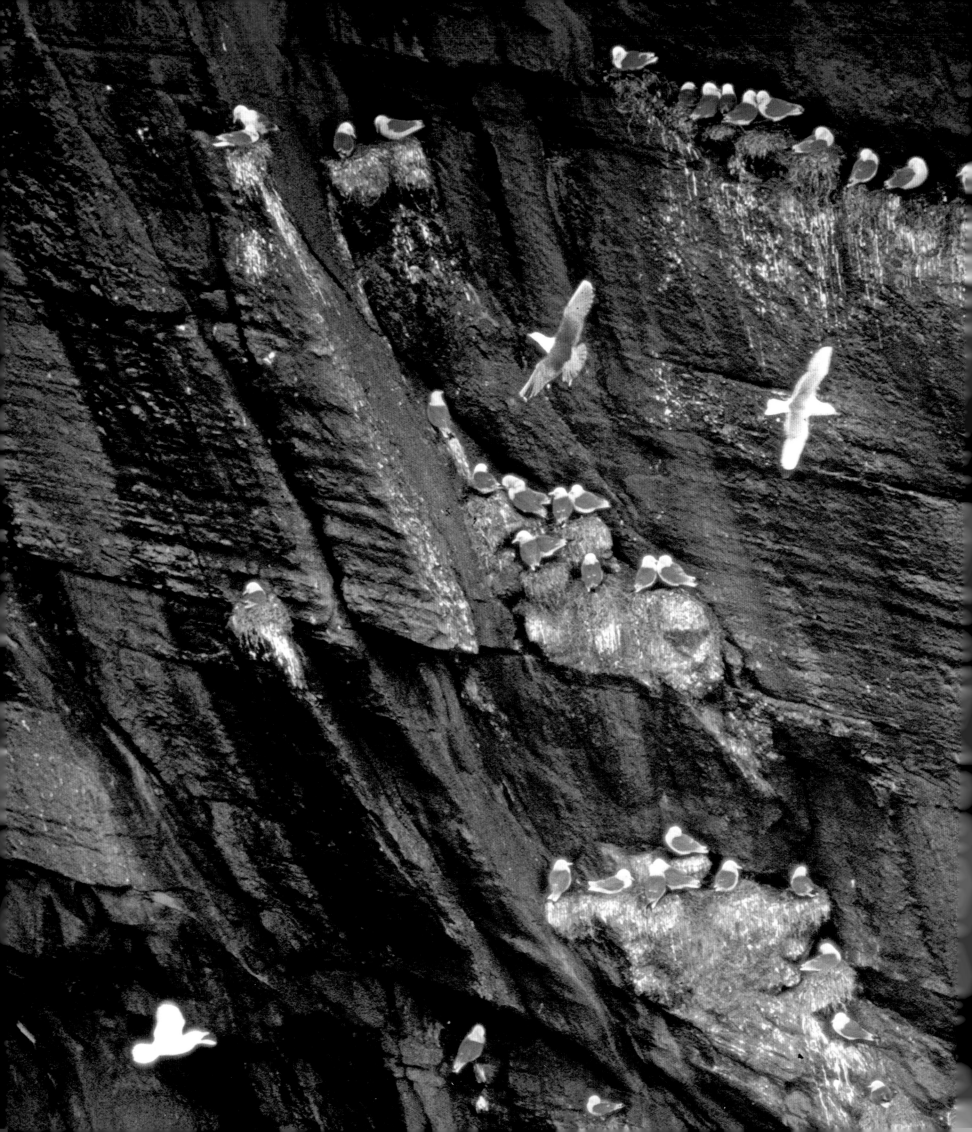

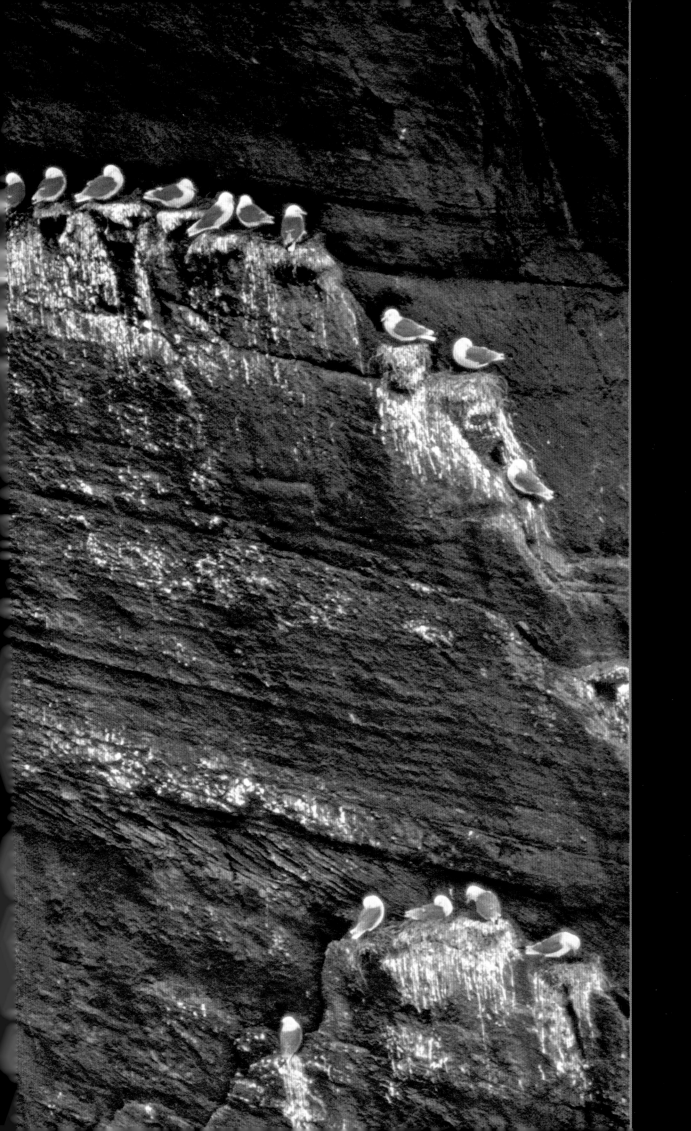

106-107 THE SLENDER LIGHTHOUSE ON
FASTNET ROCK STANDS OFF OILÉAN CLÉIRE
(CLEAR ISLAND) IN THE EXTREME SOUTHEAST
OF IRELAND. THE HELICOPTER PAD IS
INDISPENSABLE FOR DELIVERIES AND VISITS.

108-109 THE DINGLE PENINSULA'S
SHORELINE STRETCHES FOR 30 MILES INTO
THE ATLANTIC. THE COUNTRYSIDE IS GENTLE,
ARTICULATED IN BLUES AND GREENS TYPICAL
OF IRELAND'S SHORELINE.

110-111 Traditional Irish cottages are usually thatched, like this one in Inishmore.

111 A network of dry stone walls runs across the heavily eroded terrain of Inisheer, the smallest of the Aran Islands. The only easy approach to the island is from the north side, which shelves gently down to the sea.

112-113 The three-man crew of a *currach* (or *curragh*) carries the light boat ashore on Inisheer. The craft is made from tarred canvas stretched over wood.

114-115 The Aran Islands are very exposed to Atlantic storms and form a sort of protective bastion off Galway Bay, Ireland's natural "port" to the huge ocean.

116-117 BALLYNAKILL IS A SMALL
FISHING PORT IN COUNTY GALWAY
BELOW THE BARE CONICAL HILLS OF
CONNEMARA. THIS HARSH LANDSCAPE
IS SOFTENED BY THE SEA AND THE
MOORS BUT IS ONE OF THE MOST
REMOTE ON THE ISLAND.

118-119 PLACID OCEAN WAVES BREAK
ON THE ALMOST DESERTED PANORAMA
OF PORTRUSH STRAND,
COUNTY ANTRIM.

120-121 THE MAGNIFICENT
TRAWMORE BEACH, WITH THE VILLAGE
OF KEEL BEHIND IT, LIES ON ACHILL
ISLAND, THE LARGEST AND ONE OF THE
MOST INTACT OF THE ISLANDS THAT
RING IRELAND.

122-123 THE GENTLE WATERS OF THE
BAYS AND FJORDS OF COUNTY MAYO,
OR MUIGHEO, ARE SUITABLE FOR
CANOEING, AS THIS MULTICOLORED
ARRAY IN CLOGH HARBOUR
DEMONSTRATES.

124-125 ACCORDING TO LEGEND, THIS PLACID LANDSCAPE IN DOWNPATRICK HEAD, NORTH COUNTY MAYO, WAS THE SITE OF THE STRUGGLE BETWEEN ST. PATRICK AND THE DEVIL.

125 CURRAGHS, ABOUT 15 FEET LONG, DRAWN UP IN COUNTY MAYO. VERSATILE AND EASILY HANDLED, THESE BOATS SLIDE OVER THE WAVES RATHER THAN CUT THROUGH THEM.

126-127 THE RIVER BANN FLOWS INTO THE MAGNIFICENT LOUGH NEAGH IN ULSTER. THIS HUGE BODY OF WATER FILLS A NATURAL DIP IN THE GROUND JUST A FEW MILES FROM BELFAST. LEGEND DECLARES THAT THE LOUGH'S WATERS FLOWED FROM THE FOUNTAINS OF A CITY NOW SUBMERGED.

128-129 THE MORPHOLOGY OF COUNTY MAYO INCLUDES AREAS LIKE THE ALMOST DESERTED BLACKSOD BAY. THIS STRETCH OF THE COAST IS AN IMMENSE HORSESHOE-SHAPED PEAT BOG THAT LIES BETWEEN THE SEA AND THE LAND.

130-131 BLACKSOD BAY IS DESOLATE BUT SPECTACULARLY SO:
ON DAYS WHEN THE SEA IS KIND, THE SKY'S GENTLE COLORS ARE
REFLECTED IN THE WATER.

131 THE SOFT SAND OF CLONAKILTY BAY IN COUNTY CORK IS
SURROUNDED BY A DELICATE WALL OF GRAMINEOUS PLANTS.

132-133 THE WATERS THAT SURROUND IRELAND GIVE THE
LIE TO THE IDEA THAT THE NORTHERN SEAS LACK COLOR.
THE FLOW OF THE TIDES IN SLIGO BAY, ONE OF IRELAND'S
WILDEST AND MOST EXTRAORDINARY PLACES.

134-135 THE REALM OF MAN COMES TO AN ABRUPT HALT
ALONG SLIGO BAY, WHERE GEOLOGY PROVIDES A SHARP
STEP DOWN TO THE SEA.

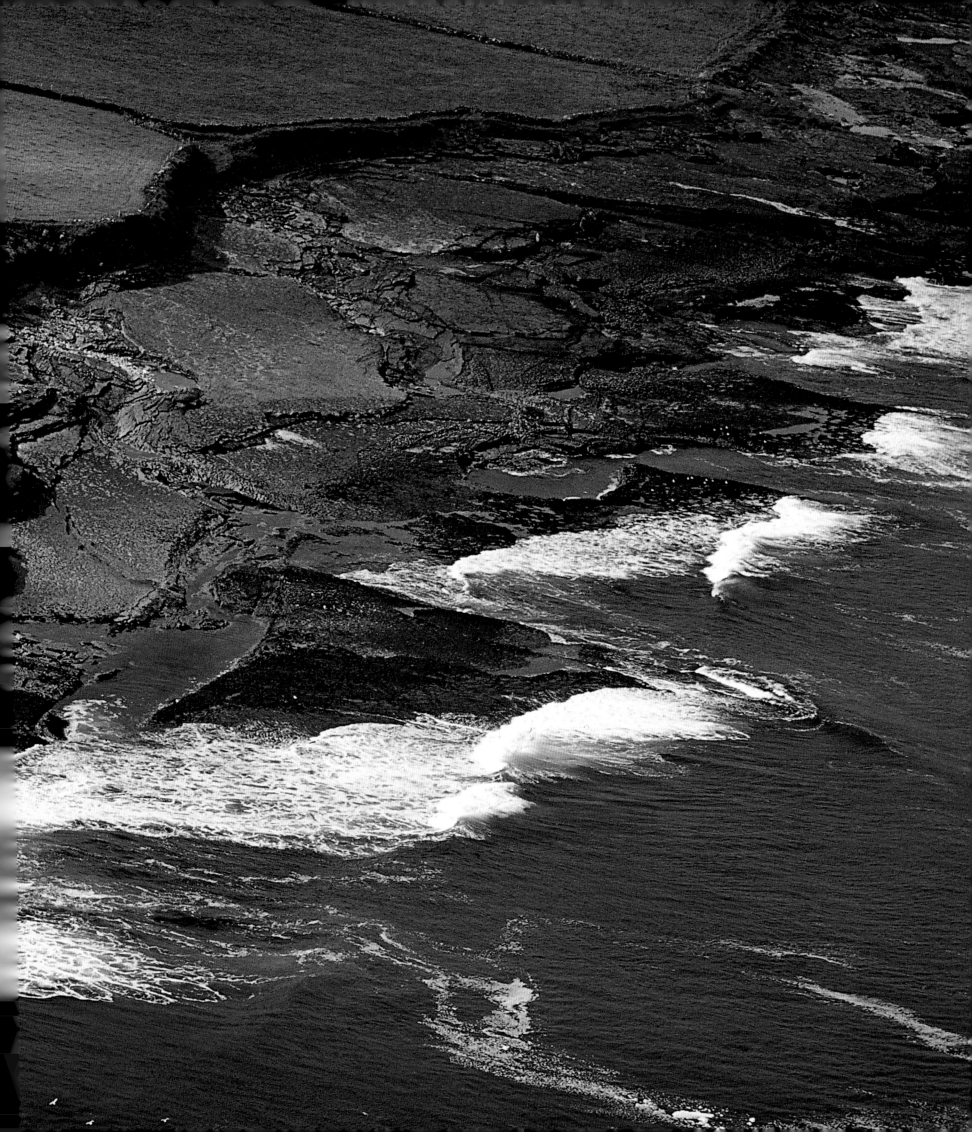

METROPOLITAN TOWNS

METROPOLITAN TOWNS

A characteristic shared by many major Irish cities and towns is their proximity to water. Most of them were founded and developed in coastal areas, on the seashore and along the estuaries of the country's rivers. Particularly significant examples of this include Dublin, on the River Liffey, which bisects the city and flows into the Irish Sea; Cork, on the River Lee; Sligo, on the River Garavogue; Limerick, on both banks of the Shannon; Kilkenny, on the banks of the River Nore; Galway, at the mouth of the Corrib; Derry, extending along the west bank of the Foyle; Belfast, lapped by the waters of the Lagan; Wexford, on the south

bank of the River Slaney; and Waterford, on the south bank of the Suir.

It is no coincidence that many of these cities were founded (or "refounded," in the case of conquests) by the Vikings, a seafaring people. Dublin itself was a Viking city established in the ninth century, while Waterford, a flourishing commercial port in the southeast, was founded by the Vikings in 853. They named it Vadrefjord, which may be translated as "Weather Shelter." It subsequently became the principal Viking settlement in Ireland.

Today Waterford is rightly famous as the "capital of crystal" and is home to the world's largest crystal glassworks, Waterford Crystal, opened in 1783 by the brothers George and William Penrose. Sligo, situated in the northwest, was occupied even earlier, in 807.

The Vikings reached Cork, in the southwest of the country, in 820, while they settled at Wexford, a city located in the southeast, in 950.

In some cases, the association with water is suggested by the very names of the cities. Dublin, for example, is derived from Dubh Linn, or "Dark Pool"; Wexford derives from Waesfjord, which means "Estuary of the Mudflats"; while Cork, coming from the word Corcaigh, may be translated as "swamp"; and Belfast, derived from Béal Feirste, as "Ford of the Sandbank."

Irish cities tend to have eventful histories, marked first by the Vikings' violent presence, and then by the Norman invasion. Subsequently, in relatively more recent times, they have been struck by bitter internecine wars. Cities in Northern Ireland, above all Derry and Belfast, still bear the scars. When walking through the streets, the visitor may come across political murals, a noted feature of the contemporary urban environment. These cities are now at a turning point, as testified by the improved situation in Belfast, which is currently enjoying a veritable urban, cultural, and social renaissance.

140 LEFT The bell tower of St. Anne's Church dominates the northern part of Cork city.

140 CENTER In 1907 the Irish crown jewels were stolen from the Bedford Tower of Dublin Castle.

140 RIGHT The Bogside is the Catholic quarter of Londonderry, the setting for dramatic and bloody events during the 1970s.

140-141 Thomond Bridge over the River Shannon leads on to King John's Castle, the fortress that King John of England built at Limerick in the 13th century.

Ireland encompasses 84,393 square km (33,753 square miles), with 70,272 square km (28,108 square miles) making up the Irish Republic, and 14,120 square km (5,648 square miles) forming Northern Ireland. The total population is about 5.6 million people, of whom 3.9 million live in the Irish Republic and 1.7 million live in Northern Ireland. More than 1 million people live in the Dublin metropolitan area, and about 300,000 live in Belfast, capital of Northern Ireland.

In recent history, the population was halved (from 8 to 4 million) by the devastating effects of the Great Famine of 1845–49. This was caused by the failure of the potato harvest in 1845, and led to mass emigration, principally to the United States, where the Irish community is still very large.

Over the last thirty years the demographic curve has begun to rise once more; the migratory flow has slowed significantly, immigration is increasing, and the birth rate has settled at one of the highest levels in Europe. As a result the country currently boasts one of the Old World's youngest populations. Ireland is Catholic stronghold in a prevalently Protestant area of Europe, and religion represents one of the principal features of the national identity. The Irish language, although it has survived the passage of time, is spoken by only a small number of the population; the dominant language is now English.

Ireland still has a largely rural economy, and only half the population lives in cities and towns. Of medium or small dimensions and, with few exceptions, only lightly industrialized, Irish cities are mainly quiet settlements, far removed from the commotion of major European metropolises, places that the visitor can still explore and be pleasantly surprised by the absence of traffic congestion.

Irish cities are on a human scale. Cork, for example, is compact but is also an attractive university town. Many places retain the appeal of medieval villages, as in the case of Kilkenny, situated in the eastern part of the Irish mid-

METROPOLITAN TOWNS

lands and traversed by the characteristic slips — narrow, winding, paved alleys that seem to lead to places beyond time. Or again, like Cork, where despite its status as the country's third-largest city after Dublin and Belfast, visitors can still enjoy pleasant strolls along the quays and bridges.

However, despite the apparent lack of bustle, Irish towns and cities are lively places, with many boasting universities. In addition to Dublin, Cork, and Galway, Limerick is another particularly important example, a vivacious, youthful place with a large student community that throngs the numerous riverside and seashore pubs along the Shannon and the coast.

At certain times of the year, however, the cities are crowded with thousands of visitors attending the country's many important cultural events and festivals. Wexford, for example, is the setting for Ireland's major Opera Festival, held every autumn, while Galway, Dublin, and Cork also stage major international events.

While many towns and cities may not be of particular architectural or artistic interest, almost all of them conserve at least one monument or building — secular or religious — that is worth visiting. Englishtown in Limerick, for example, is the oldest quarter of the city, located to the north and built in the medieval period. Known as King's Island (it is actually a true island between the Shannon and the Abbey River), it houses the thirteenth-century St. John's Castle and St. Mary's Cathedral which, erected in

1172, is the city's oldest building. The main Catholic church, St. John's Cathedral, rises in the southern part of Limerick. Built in the Gothic Revival style in 1861, it boasts Ireland's tallest church spire, soaring no less than 85 m (275 feet) high.

Many evocative places associated with the memories of artists, poets and historical figures who lived in them, welcome visitors. Sligo (a name derived from the Gaelic word *sligeach,* meaning "place of shells") is a case in point; it is a large, lively town where the celebrated poet William Butler Yeats spent his childhood summers in the company of his brother Jack. The happy, carefree times remained etched in the poet's heart and memory, and he would return to the area whenever he could. This love was reciprocal; in both the town and the surrounding area there are easily identifiable traces of his time there and of his death. At the corner of O'Connell Street and Wine Street stands the Yeats Memorial Building, the home of the Yeats Society and the Sligo Art Gallery. Each summer it hosts the Yeats International Summer School, a festival of readings and conferences on the poet's life and literary oeuvre. Close by, on the other side of Hyde Bridge, is a statue of the poet inscribed with some lines of his verse. This recognition of Yeats is just one example of how Ireland renders homage to the many artists and personalities who have distinguished a culture and history kept alive in the collective memory of the Irish people.

144 THE GILDED MORNING LIGHT COLORS THE RIVER LIFFEY, RENDERING THE HA'PENNY BRIDGE'S CURVING PROFILE ALL THE MORE SUGGESTIVE.

145 TOP LEFT CONSTRUCTION OF DUN LAOGHAIRE HARBOR BEGAN AS EARLY AS 1817; IT IS NOW ONE OF IRELAND'S MOST IMPORTANT PORTS.

145 TOP CENTER COLORFUL MARKET STALLS FLANK DUBLIN'S MOST ELEGANT SHOPS ALONG GRAFTON STREET.

DUBLIN

THE CITY OF THREE CASTLES

Those who approach Dublin from the sea have a unique opportunity to admire its magnificent position overlooking Dublin Bay and framed to the south by the peaks of the Wicklow Mountains. These offer spectacular scenery, with lakes, pools, and waterfalls dotted across the verdant valleys and moors. Further pleasures await visitors as they land; the bustling city center streets are just a short stroll away and are always crowded with people, with street artists and the young much in evidence — in fact, half of Dublin's population is under twenty-five years of age. Visitors will vouch that the youthful, lively city offers a warm welcome to all, even if many can immerse themselves in its magical atmosphere for only a few days.

Though an ancient and historic city, Dublin is also a dynamic capital and therefore in a state of continual transformation, capable of renewing itself, but also careful not to erase the memories of its past. To this end, civic groups make determined efforts to safeguard and maintain monumental and cultural heritage, rich in Georgian architecture. Visitors will note an explosive blend composed of "old traditions" and "new tendencies." Alongside a classical Dublin, the city of literary pubs and folk music, there lives a more modern city of trendy bars and rock music. The interweaving of these two realities is so complex that it is all but impossible to separate them. Juxtapositions are dramatic: A short distance away from a historic monument, an avant-garde cultural center may offer the art of tomorrow, while the street-level floors of old residential Georgian houses may sport fashionable bars. Throughout the city, new shops, cafés, and restaurants open continually. Dublin is, of course, the fulcrum of the flourishing New Economy that has earned the country the well-deserved nickname of "the Celtic Tiger." It is here, in the capital of the republic, that new ideas emerge, are developed, and contribute to the nation's visible prosperity.

145 TOP RIGHT THE BRIGHT COLORS OF HOUSE FACADES AND FRONT DOORS REFLECT DUBLINERS' EXUBERANT CHARACTERS.

145 BOTTOM IN THIS VIEW OF THE CITY AT DUSK, MODERN SKYSCRAPERS SET OFF THE CUSTOM HOUSE'S 19TH-CENTURY DOME.

146 **BOTTOM** CHRIST CHURCH CATHEDRAL (LEFT) WAS RESTORED IN 1870 AND A BRIDGE WAS BUILT TO CONNECT IT TO THE NEIGHBORING SYNOD HALL. BEDFORD TOWER (CENTER) WAS BUILT IN 1760 ON THE NORTH SIDE OF DUBLIN CASTLE, ON THE SITE OF THE ORIGINAL NORMAN ENTRANCE. (RIGHT) AFTER PASSING THROUGH TRINITY COLLEGE'S MAIN ENTRANCE, VISITORS FIND THEMSELVES AMONG STUDENTS AND PROFESSORS IN SPACIOUS PARLIAMENT SQUARE (RIGHT).

Dublin extends along both banks of the Liffey; the river bisects the city, with the division being more than merely geographical. Northside, as the city's north-bank section is called, has only recently begun coming into its own, and presents a sharp contrast to the decidedly elegant southside, which spreads out from the Temple Bar area. In the Georgian period, this was a craftsmen's and merchants' quarter, and it still retains an old-town atmosphere in the dense network of picturesque, narrow, cobbled lanes that crisscross it and give onto buildings dating back as far as the seventeenth century. Read's Cutlers, the city's oldest shop, is still there at 4 Parliament Street; it has been selling knives since 1670. The area's antiquarian flavor can also be savored to the east of the city center, in Merrion and Fitzwilliam Squares, lined by elegant Georgian buildings with shutters, wrought-iron balconies, and brightly colored front doors. Here, plaques testify to the illustrious citizens who once resided in the houses, including Oscar Wilde, W. B. Yeats, and other luminaries.

Multimedia Centre, the Project Arts Theatre, and the DESIGNyard, this last being a center for the applied arts, with exhibitions of Irish jewelry and furniture. Every evening, especially during the summer, the area is buzzing with young people thronging the pubs that serve good beer. It is perhaps no coincidence that the Guinness Storehouse, located in the original brewery where Ireland's celebrated stout is produced, is close by in the Liberties area. This is another of the city's oldest and most characteristic areas, and a medieval atmosphere still clings to the picturesque St. Thomas Road, The Coombe, Meath and James's Streets, and to the antique shops between Brick Lane and Francis Street.

Dublin's southside is also home to many of the city's major museums and civic buildings. First and foremost, Dublin Castle stands only a stone's throw from Dame Street, in the southwestern section of the city's medieval nucleus. For centuries the symbol of British authority, the castle is now used exclusively for the official ceremonies held in the luxurious State Apartments. Among these, St. Patrick's Hall contains the banners of the Knights of St. Patrick and boasts magnificent ceilings by Vincenzo Valdré, dating from 1778 and featuring symbolic representations

of the relationship between Ireland and Britain.

A short distance away on Lord Edward Street stands the City Hall, an imposing building in the Corinthian style surmounted by a cupola embellished with frescoes illustrating the history of the city. Close by soar the magnificent Catholic cathedrals of St. Patrick and Christ Church. Built by the Anglo-Norman conquerors between 1172 and 1220, Christ Church Cathedral stands on an ele-

Today, Temple Bar is a culturally and artistically lively quarter reflecting and accommodating the multifaceted initiatives of young artists. The old buildings now house modern bars and clubs, fashionable shops, and art and design galleries, and recording and television studios are to be found on every corner. Theaters, cinemas, ethnic restaurants, and cultural and multimedia centers have staked out their turf. These include the Irish Film Centre, the Arthouse

vated site overlooking the River Liffey. This cathedral was completely rebuilt between 1870 and 1880, and the crypt contains numerous objects and monuments removed and conserved during the restoration work. The central nave, in the early English Gothic style, is particularly impressive, rising 25 meters (82.5 ft.) and characterized by elegant pointed arches. A covered bridge links the cathedral to the Synod Hall. This Gothic Revival building offers residents and visitors an overview of the city's medieval history, and also exhibits Viking and Norman relics found in the nearby Wood Quay area, site of the Vikings' first settlement in Ireland. On the first floor of the Synod Hall is a scale model of Dublin, while the basement features, among other exhibits, a representation of the Black Death (the plague). Those who brave the ninety-six steps of St. Michael's Tower will enjoy a not-to-be-missed panorama.

On High Street, not far from the cathedral and framed by attractive lawns and shrubs, stands the monumental church of St. Audoen's, Dublin's oldest medieval church. It boasts a twelfth-century tower, one of the oldest (if not the oldest) in Ireland. Farther to the south, along Patrick Street on St. Patrick's Close, stands St. Patrick's Cathedral, the national cathedral of the Church of Ireland, consecrated to the country's patron saint. The first structure was erected beside a well where tradition has it that St. Patrick baptized converts around the year 450, and was nothing more than a chapel until 1192. Thereafter it was enlarged, later became a cathedral, and was subsequently transformed into the largest church in Ireland. The interior is far grander than the sober gray exterior might lead visitors to believe, and contains numerous monuments and tombs. Of note is the seventeenth-century monument to the Boyle family, Earls of Cork, with carved and painted family portraits. What is particularly striking about the interior of the cathedral is the ever-perceptible presence of the celebrated satirical writer, Jonathan Swift, who was dean of St. Patrick's from 1713 until his death in 1745. The cathedral's north transept contains Swift's Corner, with an

altar and a bookshelf with Swift's manuscripts and his funerary mask. On the southwest wall of the nave, a black plaque carries the gold-lettered inscription that Swift himself wrote: "Here lies buried the body of Jonathan Swift, dean of this cathedral, where fierce indignation can no longer rend his heart. Go, traveller, and imitate, if thou canst, one who used his utmost endeavours in the defence of liberty." Close by are the tombs of Swift and his beloved Stella. At the far west end of the cathedral rises the 43-meter (142 ft.) high Minot's Tower, in which busts, memorials, and brass plaques are conserved.

Located in the eastern part of the southside is Trinity College, the historic university founded by Queen Elizabeth I in 1591, and since then a renowned temple of learning. Trinity College's alumni include many illustrious writers, poets, dramatists, thinkers, and politicians. Among the most notable are Oliver Goldsmith, Jonathan Swift, Theobald Wolfe Tone, Edmund Burke, Bram Stoker (author of *Dracula*), J.M. Synge, James Joyce, and Samuel Beckett. The college's magnificent Old Library is still intact; it contains two million books and some five thousand manuscripts. The library's spectacular Long Room is 65 meters (215 ft.) from end to end and contains about 200,000 antiquarian texts. The Treasury is truly so named: Its priceless holdings include the *Book of Durrow* (the earliest surviving Irish illuminated manuscript), the *Book of Armagh* (a text in Latin); *The Book of Dimma* (which contains the Gospels); and the *Book of Kells* — the crown jewel of Celtic art and illumination — as well as a number of other historic liturgical texts.

Other cultural attractions in the area include Kildare Street, a short distance to the south and the site of the National Museum, the National Library, and Leinster House (home of the two chambers of the Irish parliament). Neighboring Merrion Square West has the National Gallery with Ireland's principal collection of paintings. Farther south is the verdant expanse of St. Stephen's Green, a park comprising nine gardens, water features, flower beds, and lawns.

NORTH OF THE LIFFEY

Ha'penny Bridge, the cast-iron footbridge that owes its nickname to the halfpenny toll pedestrians had to pay in the nineteenth century, connects Dublin's southside to its northside. Built by the English ironmaster John Windsor, the bridge is one of Dublin's most frequently photographed attractions; today it is enhanced by the installation of period streetlights. In recent years, the northside has been the subject of urban planning and development surveys, and a number of restoration and redevelopment projects are underway.

To the east of the bridge stretches O'Connell Street, the main street of the immediate area and in the Georgian period one of the city's most elegant; today, it is blighted by the neon signs of fast-food outlets, shopping centers, and movie theaters. A daring blend of different architectural styles, the street nonetheless still features a number of monuments and buildings of note. Among these is the General Post Office, now an important national monument because of its role in the 1916 Easter Rising. It was the site of the proclamation of the Republic of Ireland. At the far southern end of the street is the monument in honor of Daniel O'Connell, sculpted by John Foley. Known as "the Liberator," O'Connell organized a number of nonviolent campaigns in favor of the emancipation of the Irish Catholics. "The Uncrowned King of Ireland," Charles Stewart Parnell, the leader of the Home Rule movement, is honored with a statue at the northern end of the street. A short distance farther on,

Parnell Square is a kind of piazza garden, lined with recently restored eighteenth-century houses. In the center of the square stands the Rotunda Hospital. Founded in 1745, this was Europe's first purpose-built maternity hospital. Located in Parnell Square East is the Gate Theatre, which stages international contemporary productions. At 18 Parnell Square North, the Dublin Writers' Museum features a collection of first editions, rare books, letters, and mementoes of the principal Irish authors. Next door, Charlemont House contains the Hugh Lane Municipal Gallery of Modern Art, the northside's most important art gallery. Then, at 35 North Great George's Street is the James Joyce Cultural Centre, dedicated to the celebrated writer. Returning toward the river, the visitor reaches St. Mary's Pro-Cathedral on Marlborough Street, the city's Catholic cathedral. Farther south, closer to the Liffey, on Lower Abbey Street, is the Abbey Theatre, the famous national theater known for its productions of the plays of W. B. Yeats, J. M. Synge, and Sean O'Casey. Slightly farther to the east, on Custom House Quay, is the imposing Custom House. Heading westward out of central Dublin, away from the city's bustle, peace and tranquillity await in the vast Phoenix Park. Its 11-kilometer- (7-mile-) long wall encloses 700 hectares (1,730 acres), making this Europe's largest city park. With its scattering of lakes and monuments, the Zoological Gardens, and Ashtown Castle (built in the seventeenth century), Phoenix Park is unrivaled for its beauty.

152 ALONG THE CITY-CENTER STREETS, MODERN GLASS-FRONTED EDIFICES FLANK THE ELEGANT FORMS OF SOME OF DUBLIN'S OLDEST BUILDINGS.

152-153 AMONG THE BUILDINGS OVERLOOKING THE LIFFEY LOOMS THE LANTERN DOME OF THE FOUR COURTS.

154 MERRION SQUARE PRESENTS SOME OF DUBLIN'S MOST ELEGANT GEORGIAN ARCHITECTURE: THE TERRACED HOUSES RETAIN MANY OF THEIR ORIGINAL FEATURES, INCLUDING BRIGHTLY COLORED FRONT DOORS.

155 THE MONUMENT TO DANIEL O'CONNELL WAS INAUGURATED IN 1882 AT THE SOUTHERN END OF THE STREET NAMED AFTER HIM. O'CONNELL STREET IS ONE OF THE MOST IMPORTANT AND BUSIEST LINKS BETWEEN DUBLIN'S NORTHSIDE AND SOUTHSIDE.

156 AND 157 Brightly colored front doors were one of the few forms of decoration permitted by the strict rules governing architecture in the Georgian period. The result is a range of stunning tones that breaks up the severity of the dark brick facades. Each door was surmounted by a fanlight and embellished with brass knockers of various designs.

158 Dublin, a capital built on a human scale, has shops selling books and newspapers with tables where visitors can sit and
have a drink as they enjoy a break.

159 AND 160-161 Baggot Street's traditional pubs, known for their characteristic colored facades and open-air tables, are
ideal places to end the day with friends and a pint of Guinness.

162 Visitors should not make the mistake of considering Dublin's cafés and pubs as mere watering holes: They are integral to
the city's life, veritable institutions in which people meet just to chat about the day's goings-on.

163 Pipe and bowler hat: A modern, lively, and alternative Dublin contrasts with a more traditional conservative spirit.

164 AND 165 Different in period, form, style, and shape, the clocks incorporated in shop signs are a characteristic Dublin feature.

166-167 The interior of St. Patrick's Cathedral features magnificent 18th-century choir stalls. It also houses Ireland's oldest choir school, founded in 1432.

168-169 St. Patrick's nave, transepts, and aisles contain statues, busts, and epitaphs of Ireland's leading historical and cultural figures. They include Jonathan Swift, Dean of St. Patrick's from 1713.

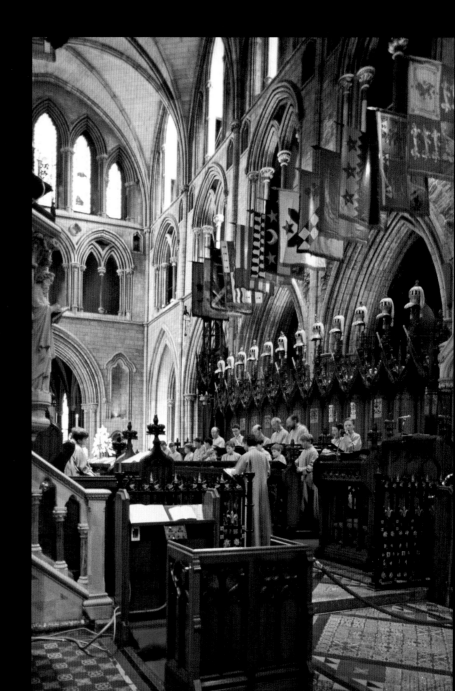

170 Parliament Square, one of the several large quadrangles within the bounds of Trinity College, contains a statue of George Salomon, the intransigent rector who between 1888 and 1904 opposed the admission of women to the historically all-male college.

170-171 On the northern side of Trinity College, visitors may admire the austere elegance of the Graduates' Memorial Building, behind which extends Botany Bay, the green area housing the university's tennis courts.

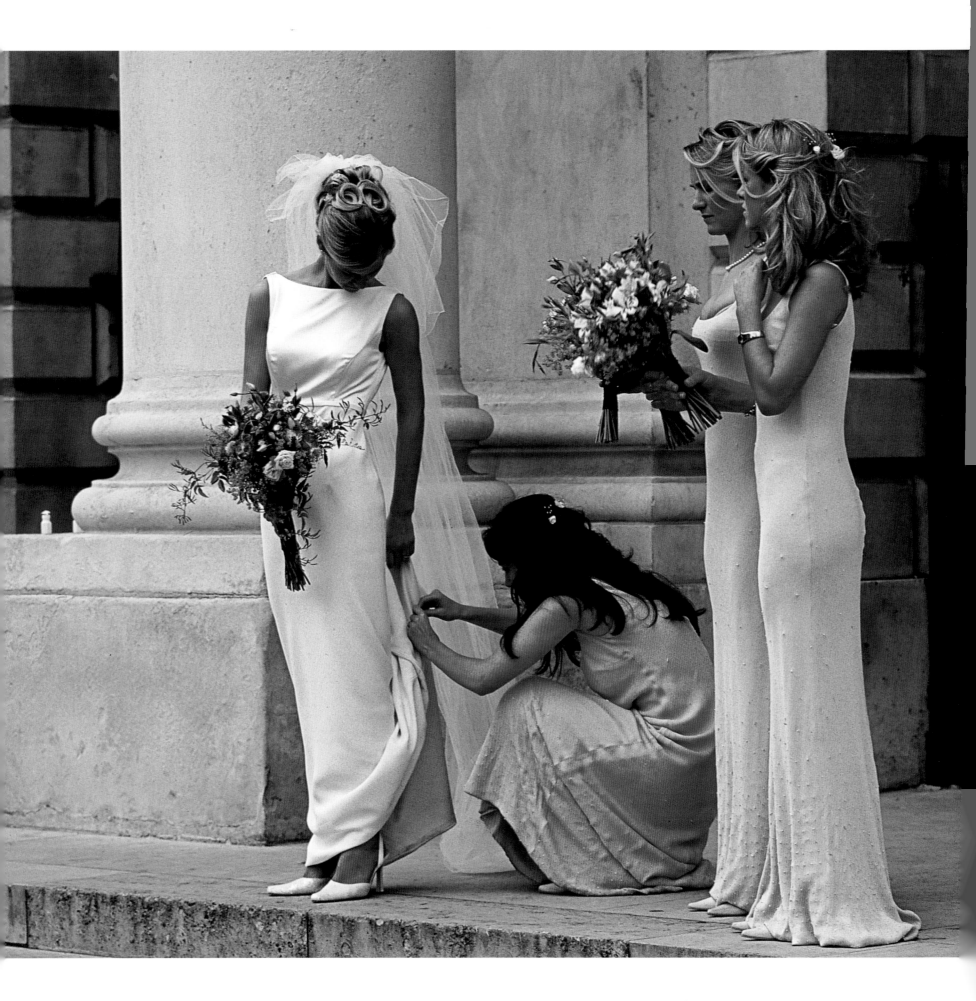

172 AND 173 The 19th-century University Chapel and the carefully tended lawns of Parliament Square create a sophisticated setting for this young couple's wedding photographs. Dubliners consider Trinity College, for centuries located in the heart of the city, to be first a municipal institution and only second a university.

174 AND 175 The Old Library's Long Room contains marble busts of illustrious Trinity College alumni such as Jonathan Swift and Edmund Burke. It also houses over 200,000 volumes and unique illuminated manuscripts such as the celebrated *Book of Kells*.

176 AND 177 The shadowy banks of the Grand Canal were the poet Patrick Kavanagh's preferred haven. In one of his poems he expressed the desire to be commemorated with a bench for passersby. Today visitors can rest alongside a bronze statue of the poet, letting their gaze wander over the placid waters.

178 St. Stephen's Green, open to the public since 1877, soon became a favorite destination for Dubliners seeking relief from the city's noise and bustle.

178-179 Work on the construction of the Grand Canal began in 1756. Designed to link Dublin with the River Shannon, the canal has gradually lost its commercial function and instead became an increasingly popular attraction for locals and for visitors.

180-181 Shortly after sunset, the first lights of the city trace the course of the River Liffey and the imposing bulk of the Four Courts.

DUBLIN'S PUBS

Dublin's famed pubs: backdrop to Irish literature's most celebrated pages, meeting places of luminaries and revolutionaries, and today not least the breeding grounds of famous rock groups. These convivial haunts may be historic or modern; they are likely to be places of literate and literary conversation, in keeping with the powerful cultural vocation that distinguishes the Irish capital. An integral part of the city's fabric, Dublin's pubs have always been far more than simple bars in which to spend an evening with friends. They are, in fact, a way of life, the Irish people's favorite place in which to meet, drink good beer, and pass the time of day. In Dublin there are plenty of pubs to choose from. At one time there were about 4,000, and while that number has been much reduced, today there are still over 1,000. First-time visitors should be aware that the word "pub" will not be found on many signs; it is far more likely that the name of the establishment will be accompanied by "inn" or "bar and lounge." For those who like to combine alcohol with culture, the Dublin Literary Pub Crawl provides a two-hour tour of the "literary" pubs, most of which are concentrated around Grafton Street. The tour introduces the places associated with the principal figures of the Irish literary tradition. At 21 Duke Street, for example, is Davy Byrne's, where James Joyce was a habitué. In *Ulysses,* he describes a Gorgonzola sandwich and a glass of burgundy that made up Leopold Bloom's lunch here. A more recent flesh-and-blood visitor to Davy Byrne's was John F. Kennedy during the time in which he was still a journalist, before he began his path to the White House, starting as a Massachusetts representative in

Congress. At the Duke Pub in Duke Street, between one pint and the next, guests can enjoy scenes staged from the works of distinguished writers such as Oscar Wilde, James Joyce, and Samuel Beckett. The Oliver St. John Gogarty, at 58–59 Fleet Street, is a pub named after a friend of Joyce's, distinguished in his own right as a surgeon, memoirist, and poet. The house hosts cultural evenings with public readings, while Saturday evenings are dedicated to traditional music. Another historic pub is McDaid's at 3 Harry Street. Its much-loved, carefully conserved Art Deco furnishings and its bohemian atmosphere recall bygone times when Patrick Kavanagh and Brendan Behan were regulars. Today it is a favored haunt of university students.

One of the best pints of Guinness in the city is served at Mulligan's, founded in 1782 at 8 Poolbeg Street. It is still lit by gas lamps and was well known to Joyce. The convivial Stag's Head at 1 Dame Court is furnished in Victorian style, but actually dates back to 1770. The oldest pub of all, however, is the Brazen Head, mentioned as a simple tavern as far back as 1198. In 1688, the city fathers granted it a license to serve as a coaching inn. The present-day pub at 20 Bridge Street Lower features dark wood paneling and dates from 1750. The Irish revolution of 1803 was apparently born here, and Robert Emmet, the legendary leader of the United Irishmen, hid in a secret room created within the building's thick walls. Concealment did him no permanent good; he was eventually betrayed and sent to the gallows. Finally, many show-business personalities favor Neary's at 1 Chatham Street, one of Dublin's most traditional pubs.

TEMPLE
BAR
Estb. 1840
EM
MALTED
GUNN
MASTERPIECE SIGNS 327277

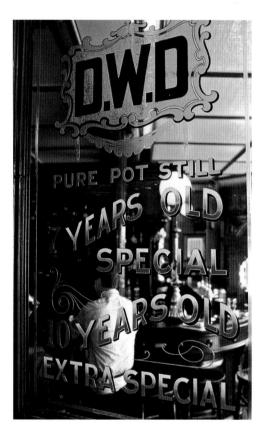

190-191 To appreciate the atmosphere of Dublin's pubs, the visitor needs to accept the idea that rather than being mere watering holes, they are an integral part of a true philosophy of life.

192-193 As well as traditional pubs with their mahogany bars, soft lighting, and carefully placed tables, there are others with more up-to-date décor but which are still permeated by that familiar atmosphere.

194-195 In the 1990s the backstreets of Temple Bar, an area that had up until this time been on the decline, became the heart of the art scene and the alternative culture of Dublin.

196 THE MURALS OF BELFAST, WHICH WERE A POPULAR MEANS OF EXPRESSION DURING THE TORMENTED YEARS OF URBAN WARFARE, HAVE NOW BECOME SYMBOLS OF NORTHERN IRELAND'S CAPITAL CITY.

197 TOP LEFT AND CENTER BELFAST'S IMPOSING CITY HALL STANDS IN THE CENTER OF DONEGALL SQUARE. ERECTED IN 1906, THE BUILDING IS COMPOSED OF A CENTRAL BLOCK AND FOUR TOWERS OVERLOOKING THE CORNERS OF THE SQUARE.

BELFAST

THE BIG SMOKE

On April 9, 1998, John Hume, the leader of the Social Democratic and Labour Party, in favor of the reunification of Ulster with the Irish Republic, and David Trimble, the representative of the Unionist parties favorable to retaining ties with Britain, signed the Good Friday Agreement. This act marked the beginning of the end of a nightmare: after twenty-five years of the Troubles, the prospect of peace had finally arisen in Northern Ireland and Belfast, its capital.

The emblem and epicenter of this rebirth was Belfast itself, long the setting for bloody armed conflict between the Catholic and the Protestant communities. The city bears the scars of the many years of civil war (as commemorated in the political murals adorning the facades of dozens of West Belfast's buildings), but indubitably an optimistic period of radical change has arrived. New buildings and office blocks are being built, modern concert and conference facilities are being developed, new stores and shop-

ping centers are being opened, and new bars and restaurants are drawing crowds. However, the true, deep-rooted change concerns the spirit of the people of Belfast and their rediscovered optimism, their obvious joie de vivre and desire to congregate in the pubs and streets, no longer to fight, but to put the past behind and enjoy a better present and a still more rewarding future.

A busy industrial city (nicknamed "Big Smoke") in County Antrim in the northeast of the country, Belfast today accounts for about a third of the total population of Northern Ireland. This is no mean feat for what just 400 years ago was a village on the River Lagan and its estuary, Belfast Lough. This location gave rise to the city's name, Béal Feirste, an Irish phrase meaning "Ford of the Sandbank."

The river has played a significant role in the history of the city, which began to expand in the early 1600s, the time of the Plantations — the policy of colonization promoted by Queen

197 TOP RIGHT SEVERE BUILDINGS LINE THE STREETS OF BELFAST, REMINDERS OF THE WEALTH THE INDUSTRIAL REVOLUTION BROUGHT TO THE CITY.

197 BOTTOM A VIEW OF WESTERN BELFAST FROM DUNVILLE PARK. THE AREA HAS RECENTLY BEEN CLEANED UP AND RESTORED TO THE CITY'S RESIDENTS AS PART OF AN EXTENSIVE URBAN RENEWAL PROGRAM FOR THE CITY'S SUBURBS.

Elizabeth I, which brought droves of Englishmen and Scots to Ireland in search of land. The country's ethnic makeup mutated rapidly, creating a population that was two-thirds Protestant and one-third Catholic. The French Huguenots who had fled their homeland after the revocation of the Edict of Nantes in 1685 denied them the right to worship soon joined the English and Scots. The French introduced new methods of working linen and contributed to the birth of a flourishing textile industry that was long one of the economic strengths of the city. Between about 1780 and 1820, Belfast saw a rapid development of its textile, engineering, and shipbuilding industries; the population expanded considerably and the first residential quarters were established as Belfast sought to confirm its status as a major city.

A number of the transformations that changed the face of the city can be seen in the Laganside port area. The old shipyards and

ter toward Belfast Lough. The many grandiose Victorian-style buildings are tangible evidence of the wealth that the industrial revolution brought to the city.

The heart of the historic inner city is a compact area that is pleasant to explore, characterized by the atmospheric Entries, a series of narrow alleys between Ann Street and High Street, the former commercial district. Located here are some of the most famous pubs, including White's Tavern (in Winecellar Entry), the oldest bar in Belfast.

A stone's-throw farther south lies the rectangular Donegall Square, Belfast's principal piazza, in the middle of which stands City Hall, a neo-Renaissance building featuring four corner towers and a huge, 53-meter- (175-ft.-) high copper dome. Taking place of honor in front of City Hall is an imposing statue of Queen Victoria in the costume of an empress. This was by no means the only monument erected to commemorate the queen after her visit in 1849, and a number of city streets and buildings were named after her. Also worthy of mention in Donegall Square is the monument commemo-

warehouses that flourished long ago but were later abandoned have given way to residential buildings and offices, linked by pedestrian walkways and attractive gardens. Then in 1997 the area further benefited from the inauguration of Waterfront Hall, an arts center with a 2,000-seat auditorium used for concerts, conferences, and exhibitions.

The River Lagan flows along the eastern side of the city cen-

rating the *Titanic,* the celebrated ocean liner that in 1912 sank on her maiden voyage to New York after striking an iceberg.

On the opposite side is a statue of Sir Edward Harland, founder of Harland & Wolff's shipyard, where the *Titanic* and her sister ship the *Olympic* were built. Standing on the north side of Donegall Square, the Linen Hall Library — the city's oldest — is well worth visiting. Founded in 1788 as the Belfast Society for

199 LEFT Belfast's City Hall was inspired by Renaissance-style models.

199 CENTER The Albert Memorial Clock Tower was built in 1861 in honor of Queen Victoria's husband.

199 RIGHT Queen's University is Ulster's most prestigious seat of learning.

Promoting Knowledge, it still features an original reading room and old stacks in dark wood holding thousands of rare and antiquarian books, the majority dealing with Irish literature and history. There is also a permanent exhibition on the history of linen.

A short distance away, between Donegall Square and Alfred Street stands the Roman Catholic St. Malachy's Church, considered to be the city's most elegant late-Georgian building. The austere redbrick exterior is in the Tudor style, while the interior, is highly decorated and features a rococo stucco ceiling.

Farther north, on the corner of Donegall Street and Talbot Street, stands St. Anne's Cathedral, the Anglican Church of Ireland's most important center of worship. Rather than its neo-Romanesque exterior, St. Anne's is known for its interior, which features colorful mosaics created in the 1920s.

The enormous example covering the baptistery ceiling is composed of 150,000 pieces. The broad central nave with its floor in Canadian maple is also attractive. In contrast, the aisles are paved with Irish marble. Lord Carson, the formidable foe of Home Rule and promoter of Irish Partition, is buried in the south aisle.

In Queen's Square, situated just to the southeast, stands the Albert Memorial Clocktower, erected in 1869 in memory of Queen Victoria's prince consort.

A few meters to the west of Donegall Square winds Great Victoria Street, the hub of a series of central streets known as the Golden Mile, an area in which the contrast between old and new is most evident.

Typically, alongside the sumptuous Victorian Grand Opera House, designed by the well-known theater architect Frank Matcham, rise the towers of the renovated Europa Hotel. Modern cafés and restaurants offering specialities from throughout the world flank the historic Crown Liquor Saloon, a pub celebrated for its polychrome tile facade. A few meters to the west of Great Victoria Street is Sandy Row, the principal street of a Protestant working-class district. Its many murals depicting armed men are a significant example of the different worlds that coexist within Belfast.

Just to the south lie the university quarters, concentrated around Queen's College, built in 1849. Unlike Trinity College, Dublin, with its largely Classical-style buildings, Queen's College is basically Tudor in style, with traditional red-toned brickwork, not unlike Magdalene College, Cambridge. Renamed Queen's University after a major expansion, it is now Northern Ireland's most prestigious seat of learning, a cosmopolitan institution that also stages musical events and art exhibitions. Leaving the university and heading south, visitors encounter the lively Botanic Gardens with the magnificent Palm House, a huge glass and cast-iron greenhouse with temperate and tropical zones in which, among others specimens, many carnivorous plants are grown. At the edge of the park stands Ulster Museum, with its collections of ancient objects and manufactures. Among its most valuable treasures are the gold and silver coins and objects recovered from the *Girona,* the famous Spanish Armada ship that sank off the Giant's Causeway in 1588.

Lastly, there are the two working-class quarters of Shankill Road (Protestant) and Falls Road (Catholic), two still-tense districts once divided by the so-called Peace Line. The visitor will note the protest murals and the colors of the British flag (red, white, and blue) and those of Irish flag (green, white, and orange) painted on the pavements, commemorating the once-ferocious hostilities.

However, given the many signals that the city is working toward a rewarding future, these symbolic reminders of the troubled past are fortunately of little import.

200 A MONUMENT TO THE *TITANIC* AND THE VICTIMS OF HER TRAGIC MAIDEN VOYAGE STANDS ON THE EAST SIDE OF CITY HALL. HARLAND & WOLFF, FROM WHOSE SHIPYARD THE CELEBRATED LINER WAS LAUNCHED, WAS AT THE TIME ONE OF THE CITY'S MOST PROSPEROUS FIRMS.

201 AND 202-203 THE ARCHITECTURAL DETAILS OF CITY CENTER BUILDINGS AND THE AUSTERE LINES OF ULSTER BANK EVOKE MEMORIES OF BELFAST'S GLORY AS NORTHERN IRELAND'S CAPITAL DURING THE INDUSTRIAL REVOLUTION.

204-205 THE CROWN LIQUOR SALOON, THE CITY'S OLDEST PUB, WAS BUILT IN 1880. THE OPULENCE OF ITS POLYCHROME FACADE WITH MOSAICS OF COLORED TILES IS REPEATED INSIDE, WITH AN INTERIOR DOMINATED BY THE MAHOGANY BAR AND EMBELLISHED WITH FRESCOES, STAINED GLASS, AND A SCROLLED CEILING.

206 AND 207 THE POWERFUL LINES OF BELFAST CITY HALL DOMINATE THE CITY CENTER.
THANKS TO ITS GRANDIOSE CENTRAL DOME (175 FT. HIGH), IT CAN BE SEEN FROM ALL DIRECTIONS.
THE DOME IS CLAD WITH COPPER AND INTERNALLY FEATURES RARE ITALIAN MARBLE.

208-209 Two children playing in the street in the Catholic area of Belfast, close to the Peace Wall. The curving wall, which is clearly visible in the photograph above, divides the Catholic and Protestant areas on the city's outskirts. British troops erected the wall in 1969 in an attempt to subdue the bloody skirmishing between the two factions.

210-211 What identifies these two murals as Loyalist political messages is the red fist, the symbol of the province of Ulster since medieval times.

212-213 This statue made by John Kindness in 1999 is known as the Big Fish. It was commissioned in celebration of the redevelopment of the Waterfront area on the River Lagan. The "skin" of the fish is made of ceramics decorated with images and texts relating to Belfast's history. The sculpture and the facade of the Trade Union Building (above), featuring an abstract mosaic of colored tiles, are examples of the architectural vivacity of a city that is freeing itself from the specters of the past.

214 AND 215 1997 saw the inauguration in Laganside (the River Lagan's old port area) of Waterfront Hall, a cultural center with an auditorium that has become a symbol of the architectural fervor revolutionizing Belfast's appearance and progress.

LONDONDERRY

THE OAKS OF SAINT COLUMBA

Londonderry is the administrative center of County Derry (or Londonderry). It is situated at the inland end of Lough Foyle, and extends along the west bank of the River Foyle, which flows into the *lough* or "lake." To the southeast the city is framed by the gentle, rounded Sperrin Mountains and to the north and west by the majestic peaks of Donegal. The city is Ireland's fourth largest, and in Northern Ireland is second only to Belfast, the capital, although the two are very close in terms of size.

Originally, the city was called Derry, a toponym derived from *Daire Calgaig,* which translates literally as the "Oak Grove of Calgach," Calgach being the warrior chieftain of the Caledonians (i.e., the Scots) during the Battle of the Grampians. The name persisted for centuries, apparently long after 546, when St. Colombanus founded a monastery here and the settlement was re-baptized as Doire Cholmcille. At the beginning of the seventeenth century, during the Plantations (the influx of colonists), the town began to transform into a small commercial center, and the term "Doire" was Anglicized as "Derry." The prefix "Lon-

don" was added in 1613 in order to underline the ties with the Twelve Companies of the Corporation of London, to which Derry was subject. "Derry" and "Londonderry" are not therefore two names by which the city can be called indifferently: Used by local Catholics (who constitute two thirds of the total population) and by Protestants, the different names can represent precise political declarations. However, debate over the origin of the city's name reflects only one factor in its turbulent history.

Proudly known to its inhabitants as "the Maiden City," Londonderry is well known for the bloody battles and long sieges it survived without ever having been taken. In 1689 James II's Catholic troops laid siege to Londonderry. This determined effort lasted 105 long days (a record for the British Isles), but the city remained undefeated. In the 1970s, Londonderry became the setting for extremely violent armed conflicts between British troops and Catholic separatists. However, neither in the distant past nor in more recent times has Derry ever shown any sign of giving way, continuing to resist to the cry of "No

216 Behind the buildings lining Magazine Street can be seen the O'Doherty Tower, home of the Tower Museum. It is Londonderry's most important museum and offers a multimedia presentation of the city's troubled history.

217 BOTTOM Many homeowners in the Catholic quarter transformed the facades of their houses into political propaganda displays during the violent 1970s.

LONDONDERRY: THE OAKS OF SAINT COLUMBA

surrender!" It now looks proudly back at its history and the courage that distinguishes it, finding the strength to turn the page and yet again rebuild its fortunes. The old town is still surrounded by its seventeenth-century defensive walls, pierced by the four historic portals of Shipquay, Butcher, Bishop, and Ferryquay. Over 6 meters (20 ft.) high and up to 9 meters (30 ft.) wide at certain points, with a perimeter of around 1.6 km (1 mile), the walls are still in excellent condition and represent one of the best examples of old military fortifications in Europe. While these walls are clearly visible, other invisible barriers separate the Catholic and Protestant (Loyalist) inhabitants of a city that still bears the scars of the sectarian hostility. An example is the Bloody Sunday Memorial in the Catholic Bogside quarter (located just beyond the old city walls past Butcher's Gate) commemorating the Derry victims of January 30, 1972, when 13 unarmed citizens protesting for equal rights were killed in cold blood by troops from the British Parachute Regiment. This monument is by no means the only testimony to those difficult years, the so-called Troubles. Visitors walking around in this quarter will frequently encounter political murals of accusation and protest. Prominent among them is the celebrated sign at the entrance to Bogside that reads "You are now entering Free Derry." Other examples are the murals in Lisfannon Park referring to the celebrated Republican activist Bernadette Devlin (McAliskey). A number of these murals are so accomplished that they are now regarded as works of art: Among them are the Psychedelic Rainbow and other celebrated examples in Meenan Square. The Protestant Loyalists also use this form of expression, but with opposing slogans and messages. Their murals can be found throughout the city's Protestant areas, including Bond Street, Irish Street, Lincoln Courts, Nelson Drive, and The Fountain. On London Street, at the highest point in the city, stands the Anglican St. Columbanus's Cathedral, built between 1628 and 1633 in a somewhat modernized Gothic

style. The bell tower, once used as a lookout post, offers the finest views out over the old town. The Chapter House contains keys and locks used to seal the city during the famous siege of 1689, and the vestibule features a cannonball fired by the besieging forces, conveying the British conditions for surrender. The cathedral's stained glass windows illustrate episodes from St. Columbanus's mission in England, as well as the much later siege of the city. From the cathedral visitors can walk down toward Bishop's Street Within. This street, which is lined by elegant buildings, bisects Derry's historic center. The heart of the city is marked by its main square, known as "the Diamond," which contains a monument of the same name commemorating the dead of the First World War. Leading off the Diamond to the left is Butcher Street, where the Calgach Genealogy Centre is to be found. Its "Fifth Province" feature allows visitors to participate in a multimedia exploration of the history and culture of Ireland. Also leading off the Diamond is the steep Shipquay Street, lined by impressive commercial buildings. At the far end of this street, and well worth a visit, is the Derry Craft Village. This is a faithful reproduction of a typical stone-built Irish village, with a maze of lanes and a small central square around which are set buildings restored to their traditional style, with cafés and shops. Opened in 1992, the Craft Village is part of a city center redevelopment project. A little farther on, just before the boundary of the city walls, is the O'Doherty Tower on Union Hall Place that houses the Tower Museum. There another multimedia presentation recounts the story of Derry from its foundation to the Troubles. Beyond the walls, the Guildhall, built in 1890, stands on Guildhall Square, overlooking the river. It boasts a finely decorated facade with a corner tower and a four-faced clock. The stained glass windows (copies of the originals) illustrate the history of Derry. Just behind the Guildhall is Derry Quay, from which Irish emigrants set sail for the New World in the eighteenth and nineteenth centuries.

220 AND 221 Within the imposing City Walls is the old town of Derry, characterized by examples of recently restored and brightly painted 19th-century architecture.

222-223 AND 224-225 Examples of an exquisitely popular art form, the murals of Londonderry are the city's most celebrated symbols. The most recent of them, brightly colored and decorating shop windows and the facades of clubs, sit alongside those commemorating the dramatic Bloody Sunday episode, a tragic day in which British soldiers shot and killed 13 unarmed Catholic protesters.

226 AND 227 The most beautiful and significant of the city's murals are those in the Catholic quarter; they express residents' anger at the violence they have suffered and celebrate their heroes, such as the activist Bernadette Devlin.

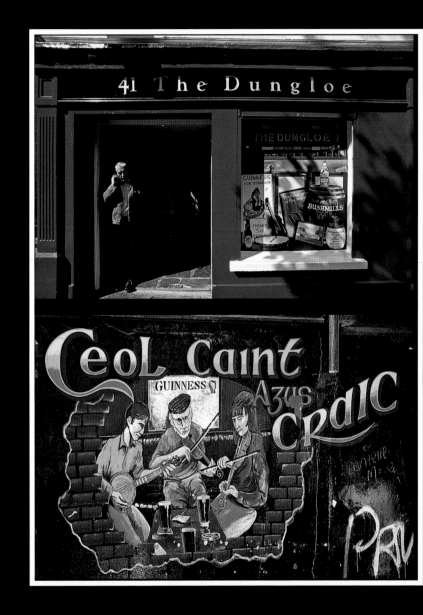

An enchanting university town in the southwest of Ireland, Cork is truly a city built on the human scale. A county town and an important commercial center, it is welcoming with a familiar, somewhat romantic air. Its name derives from the Irish word *Corcaigh,* meaning "swamp," and the city's origins date back to the seventh century, when St. Finbarr founded an abbey on the site where the majestic neo-Gothic cathedral dedicated to him now stands. Since the city's foundation, its history has always been fairly lively. The Vikings sacked and pillaged Cork in 820; the Normans invaded it in the twelfth century. In more recent times, the city suffered violence in the Anglo-Irish war and the civil war; in fact, Michael Collins, the famous political leader who fought for Ireland's independence after the 1916 Easter Rising, was killed in an ambush outside Cork. Today the atmosphere is very different and Cork is in the spotlight only dur-

ing the annual Film Festival, held in early October, and during the Jazz Festival, held at the end of that same month. However, the city is well worth visiting at any time of the year.

The ideal place to start exploring Cork is its historic center, built on a narrow island between the two channels of the River Lee. As it flows away from the center, the Lee splits into numerous channels and its estuary constitutes one of Europe's largest natural harbors. In fact, until the nineteenth century, Cork resembled a Dutch city, thanks to the number of navigable waterways running through it.

Today, it is very pleasant to stroll along the narrow medieval lanes, the famous quays, and the city center's attractive bridges. Grand Parade, the principal thoroughfare traversing the area, boasts attractive late-eighteenth-century buildings with rounded facades finished with slabs of gray slate, as well as the National Monument,

CORK

THE CAPITAL OF THE SOUTH

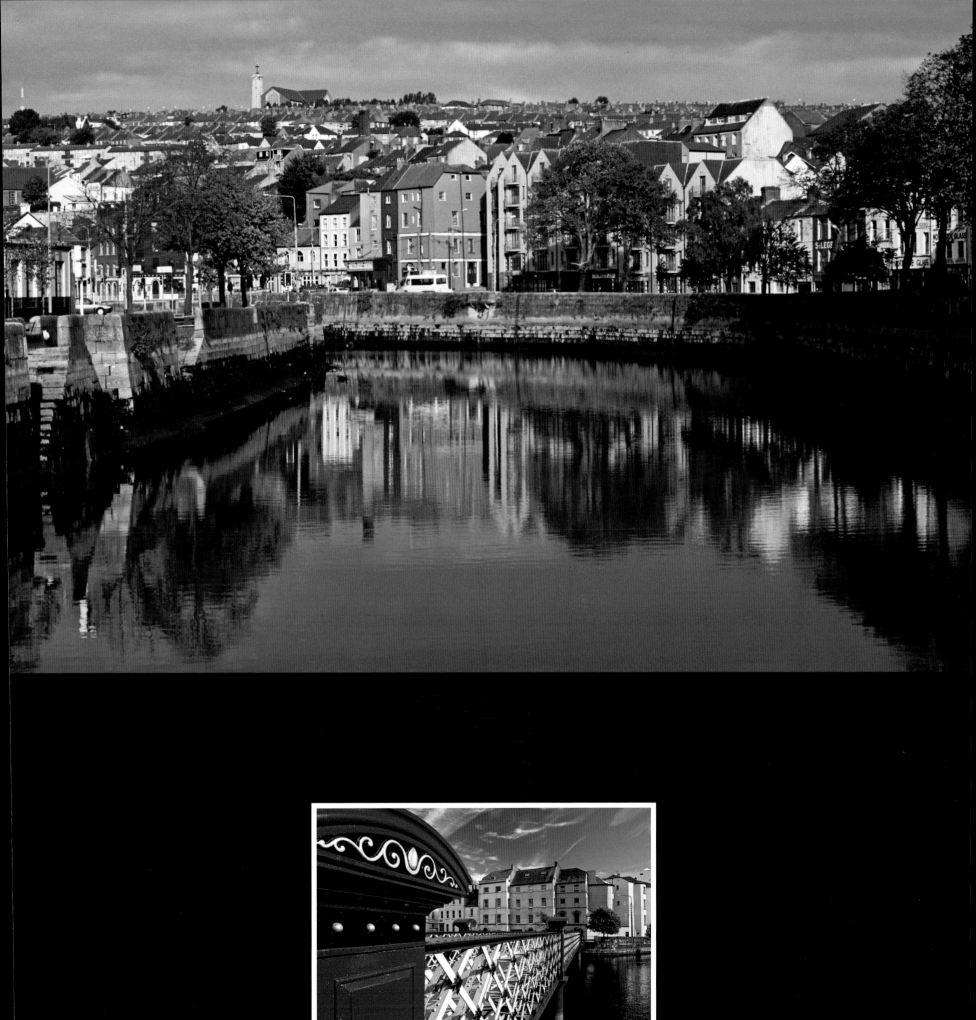

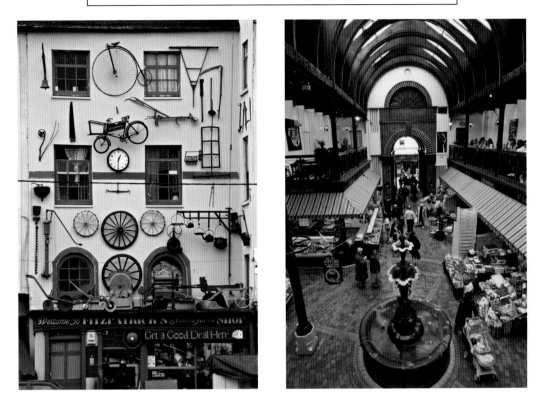

230 AND 231 LEFT These shop facades will hardly pass unnoticed: Well-stocked shelves decorate this shop specializing in textbooks while antique bicycles, a clock, and assorted gardening tools and kitchen implements distinguish Fitzpatrick's Second Hand Shop on George's Quay.

231 RIGHT The English Market is a Cork institution: The first historical references to this lively covered market in the city center date as far back as 1610.

commemorating the patriots who fell in the pro-independence insurrections that occurred between 1798 and 1867. Between Grand Parade and Princes Street is the interesting covered English Market, selling local sea and farm specialties and other fresh produce. Grand Parade also intersects with St. Patrick's Street, which offers a range of large stores and smaller speciality stores. About 100 meters (330 ft) away, the colorful stalls of the daily Coal Quay flea market, held along Cornmarket Street, provide a contrast with the elegant store-window displays of St. Patrick's Street. Close by is Paul Street, renowned for its ethnic restaurants, sophisticated cafés, trendy boutiques, and well-stocked bookstores. Leading off Cornmarket Street are the lively French Church Street and Carey's Lane, crammed with bars, pubs, restaurants, and vintage clothing stores. This is also the district favored by the county's artistic and intellectual elite as a residential area.

The liveliest part of the city is the port area which, especially in the summer, transforms into an open-air stage where street performers demonstrate their talents. In a quiet corner of the city, to the south of the River Lee on Bishop Street, stands majestic St.

Finbarr's Cathedral. Completed in 1878 to the designs of the noted William Burges, the cathedral features stained glass windows illustrating episodes from the life of Christ. Alongside St. Finbarr's is Elizabeth Fort, and close by to the east are the remains of Red Abbey, a thirteenth-century Augustinian monastery, carefully maintained as the city's oldest building.

On Cork's outskirts, overlooking the center from the north, is the Montenotte district, one of Cork's most elegant residential areas and once home to wealthy Victorian families. It is reached via the Christy Ring Bridge toward Pope's Quay. Just before the bridge, Emmet Place, a brick and limestone building dating from 1724, houses the Crawford Municipal Art Gallery, repository of the city's principal art collections. On the far side of the bridge stands St. Mary's Dominican Church, but the area is dominated by the imposing cathedral of St. Anne's Shandon. Built in 1722, the cathedral features two sandstone and two limestone facades. Locals affectionately call the clock mounted in the tower the "four-faced liar" and with good reason; until it was repaired in 1986, each of the four dials showed a different time.

232 AND 233 SOME OF CORK'S BUILDINGS PRESENT AN IMAGINATIVE
DECORATIVE DETAILING DISPLAYED IN COLORS AND FORMS. ON THE
FACADE OF THIS HOUSE ST. PATRICK IS SEEN RIDDING THE ISLAND OF
SNAKES. THE SIDE OF A HOUSE ON A STREET CORNER THOUGHTFULLY
CURVES TO FOLLOW A BEND IN THE STREET.

234 St. Mary's Dominican Church overlooks Pope's Quay. The church contains a 15th-century statute dedicated to Our Lady of Grace that for centuries has been attributed with miraculous powers.

235 Small painted metal shop signs, old-style street lamps, and colorfully decorated houses enliven the streets of the city center.

236 TOP Ireland's fourth largest city, Galway grew from a fishing village and still features the traditional fishing boats of its past, known in Gaelic as *PUCANS* and *GLEOITEOGS*.

236 BOTTOM Galway's streets boast rows of old shops with wood and stone facades.

237 TOP LEFT Known locally as simply "The Square," Eyre Square is the heart of Galway.

GALWAY

THE GATEWAY TO THE WEST

A lively university city, Galway attracts a myriad of young people who flock there during the academic year. In the summer, it is host to an ever-increasing number of tourists, particularly during the last two weeks of July. Then the Galway Arts Festival — the country's premier arts event, featuring music, dance, plays, street theater, and much, much more — is in full swing.

The serious matter of fine food also draws visitors, and every September gourmets descend on the attractive fishing port for its international Oyster Festival, famous for over half a century as a mouth-watering, appetite-satisfying occasion.

Galway dates back to the late thirteenth century, when the Anglo-Norman Burke family founded a settlement on the River Corrib's eastern bank. Today it is western Ireland's largest city, with a population of around 60,000, and it is the administrative center of the county of the same name.

On the River Corrib's west bank, beyond the Spanish Arch, stands the Claddagh, a picturesque fishing village founded long before the arrival of the Normans. The village has changed and the characteristic white thatched-roof cottages no longer exist, having gradually been replaced by modern terraced housing. Nonetheless, visitors to the area will inevitably hear talk of the Claddagh ring that has ensured the village's fame throughout the country. The ring takes the form of two hands (symbol of friendship) clasping a heart (symbol of love and passion) and surmounted by a crown (loyalty). Tradition has it that the ring was designed in Claddagh. The legend recounts that a man named Richard Joyce, just about to be married, was instead kidnapped by ruthless slavers and carried off to Africa. There he learned to design and make jewelry, including a ring he wished to give to the woman he was to have married. Joyce earned his master's favor, and this man offered Joyce his wealth and his daughter's hand in marriage. But Joyce still hoped to return to Claddagh and find his Irish love. After many years he was able to, and finally became reunited with his fiancée, who (in the best traditions of true love) had remained faithful to him. Joyce presented her with the ring he had designed and made,

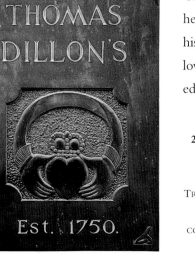

237 TOP CENTER AND RIGHT Galway's city center is situated on the River Corrib's banks and is characterized by narrow streets lined with numerous pubs.

237 BOTTOM The motif of Claddagh ring, a heart enclosed by two hands, is the subject of a legend documented as far back as the 18th century. Tradition has it that the heart should be worn facing the fingertips if the wearer has yet to find a companion and toward the hand as an engagement or wedding ring.

239 TOP LEFT The characteristic Galway boats featured in the city's coat of arms were used to carry turf and beer.

239 TOP RIGHT Crossing the river over the Salmon Weir bridge, visitors reach the modern Cathedral of St. Nicholas.

239 BOTTOM The city center's winding streets were carefully restored in the 1970s.

240-241 The Corrib is a fairly short river; virtually its entire length is within the city bounds, lending a poetic touch to every view.

and presumably the couple lived happily ever after. Today, the center of Galway extends along the banks of the River Corrib, which flows south from Lough Corrib into the broad Galway Bay. The town's central area is still traversed by narrow, twisting medieval streets. Fortunately, when urban renewal projects began in the 1970s, these streets were restored along with the rest of the city, rather than falling victim to clearance. The newer section of Galway is centered on Eyre Square, to the east of the river. It encloses a small park surrounded by imposing nineteenth-century buildings and a number of monuments. From Eyre Square, William Street and Shop Street lead to the lively Latin Quarter. On the corner of Abbeygate Street Upper and Shop Street stands the city's most impressive sixteenth-century building, Lynch's Castle, once the home of the powerful Lynch family. Gargoyles, ornaments, and medallions decorate the building's gray stone facade, giving a certain grandeur to the bank it now houses. Close by is the Collegiate Church of St. Nicholas, specifically, St. Nicholas of Myra, patron saint of sailors. Founded in 1320 and rebuilt and enlarged on a number of occasions during the

fifteenth and sixteenth centuries, the church is Galway's finest medieval building, and its fifteenth-century West Porch is decorated with elegant relief sculptures. A number of interesting tombs can be found inside, and the south transept was extended to house the Lynch Memorial, which commemorates an episode from the fifteenth century. Tradition has it that James Lynch, a judge of the time, sentenced his son Walter to death for murder and then performed the execution himself, as no one else was willing to do so. Farther to the south lies Quay Street, lined with bars and restaurants, while a short distance away, close to the Old Quays, the Spanish Arch can still be admired. It marks the area where Spanish traders once unloaded goods from their ships. To the north of the city, beyond the Salmon Weir Bridge, rises the Cathedral of St. Nicholas, a Catholic church consecrated to the Assumption of Our Lady and St. Nicholas. Designed by John Robinson in 1957, it was built in local limestone and Connemara marble. Farther to the west lies University College of Galway, where a modern campus has been built around the original neo-Gothic buildings.

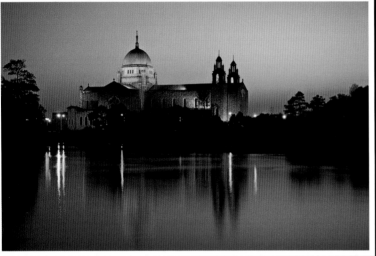

242 THE SEVERITY OF THE SCHOOL UNIFORMS CONTRASTS WITH THESE LADS'
LAUGHTER. KILKENNY COLLEGE, AN INSTITUTION DATING BACK TO 1666,
SAFEGUARDS THE CITY'S CULTURAL TRADITIONS.

243 **TOP LEFT AND CENTER** KILKENNY HAS TWO CATHEDRALS,
ST. MARY'S (LEFT) AND ST. CANICE'S (CENTER). ST. MARY'S WAS BUILT IN THE
19TH CENTURY WHILE THE FIRST HISTORICAL REFERENCES TO ST. CANICE'S
DATE FROM 1087.

KILKENNY

INDEPENDENT BY NATURE

Alice Kyteler has long been a subject of speculation in southeastern Ireland. She lived during the Middle Ages and was commonly known as "the Witch of Kilkenny." Although she survived no fewer than four husbands, all of whom died in mysterious circumstances, this was not the reason for accusations of witchcraft. In fact, the first suspicions to be aired dated back to a period in which she had made enemies of a number of powerful figures. It was then that gossips swore they had seen her make sacrifices and pacts with the devil. As was all too common at the time, the people closest to Alice also paid a price and were sentenced to death. Alice fled to England, and her son William is known to have survived, but nothing is known of her sister's fate. It is on record that Alice's maid Petronella was actually burned at the stake. Today, the house in which Alice once lived (27 Saint Kieran's Street) has been transformed into Kyteler's Inn, a bar and restaurant.

Despite its storied past, Kilkenny, a county seat, remains

one of the most enchanting inland Irish towns, located in the eastern part of the republic's southern midlands, not far from Cashel. A proud, compact town, Kilkenny has not let progress destroy the magic of the past; modernity and tradition manage to coexist quite happily. Much of the appeal of a medieval village remains, fully apparent in the narrow stone-flagged "slips," or alleys. These are overlooked by medieval black-stone buildings, which are enlivened by colorful store facades and painted signs.

The town is divided into three distinct districts, with the Irishtown quarter lying to the north. Here, at the top of the hill of the same name and at the end of Parliament Street, stands the triple-naved St. Canice's Cathedral, dating back to the mid-thirteenth century and considered to be one of Ireland's most beautiful old churches. Inside, walls clad in dark local marble contrast strongly with the pale sandstone pillars. The floor in polychrome tiles features four different types of marble: Connemara green,

243 **TOP RIGHT** KILKENNY CASTLE,
AN ANCIENT NORMAN FORTRESS, IS
TODAY A BULWARK OF ARTISTIC
EXPRESSION, HOUSING WITHIN ITS WALLS
THE KILKENNY DESIGN CENTRE AND
THE BUTLER ART GALLERY.

243 **BOTTOM** ARTISTS WORKING IN
KILKENNY CAN MAKE USE OF A
WIDESPREAD BLACK LIMESTONE THAT
HAS EARNED IT THE NICKNAME OF THE
"MARBLE CITY."

244 The colorful buildings lining High Street catch the attention of visitors glancing out from the Slips, the narrow and shadowy lanes of medieval Kilkenny.

245 LEFT AND RIGHT Red, blue, yellow: the doors of the city's pubs and shops provide continual chromatic surprises.

KILKENNY, INDEPENDENT BY NATURE

Cork red, Tyrone grey, and Kilkenny black. The cathedral contains a number of impressive sixteenth-century tombs embellished with bas-reliefs in black marble. The main building is flanked by the Round Tower, built in the sixth century and standing 30 meters (100 ft.) high. The top of the tower offers a breathtaking panorama of Kilkenny.

St. Canice's steps lead down from the cathedral southward to Dean Street. From here, Parliament Street leads toward the central High Town quarter. High Street, the main thoroughfare in this area, is lined with old buildings including the Tholsel, or City Hall, that features an attractive arcade and is topped by a Clock Tower. Rothe House, the Tudor resi-

dence of a wealthy merchant family, is to be found in Parliament Street. Today it is the home of Kilkenny Museum (containing a small costume gallery and an exhibit of archaeological finds); it also houses the library of Kilkenny Archaeological Society. Farther down is Watergate Theatre, which presents dramas, comedies, and musicals. There are also a number of pubs on Parliament Street, above all Smithwick's brewery-pub where for three centuries one of the finest and best-known Irish bitters has been brewed. The Guinness group has given the name "Kilkenny" to one of its celebrated beers.

In Blackmill Street, which runs parallel to Parliament Street, stands the Catholic cathedral of St. Mary's, flanked by a 61-meter (200-ft.) tower. Built in 1857 in the Gothic style, the cathedral is situated close to Black Abbey, a building dating from 1225. The abbey, named after the color of the monks' habits, is the city's best-loved church. Dominating the area and flanked by extensive

grounds overlooking the River Nore is Kilkenny Castle, one of Ireland's most famous fortresses. The first building on the site of this imposing Norman castle was erected by the conqueror Strongbow in 1190. During the last century, it was rebuilt in the Gothic Revival style and was recently restored. The cylindrical towers and massive walls of the original medieval design have sur-

vived. One of the most attractive of the castle's many rooms is the Long Gallery, lit by a glazed roof supported on wooden beams. The painted ceiling panels feature decorative motifs taken from the illuminated Gospel manuscripts painted by the monks of Kells (whose *Book of Kells,* now conserved at Trinity College, Dublin, was described earlier).

The castle's old stables have been transformed into Kilkenny Design Centre, an exhibition and sales facility where visitors may see craftsmen at work and may purchase their products. A suite of the former servants' rooms houses Butler Contemporary Art Gallery.

Across John's Bridge, on the other side of the River Nore, lies Kilkenny's eastern district. A striking series of windmills, many still in working order, is a feature of this area. Kilkenny College, famous for having Jonathan Swift among its alumni, was situated in Lower John Street untill 1985.

246 AND 247 COUNTY KILKENNY OFFERS MYRIAD VARIATIONS ON GREEN TURF AND WAYS OF ENJOYING IT: THE VISITOR CAN TAKE UP THE CURVED STICK FOR A HURLING MATCH OR VENTURE INTO A GARDEN WITH NOTHING MORE DEMANDING IN MIND THAN RELAXING WITH A GOOD BOOK.

GAELICSPIRIT

248 CLOCKWISE How can the spirit of the Irish be illustrated in pictures? By showing their love for horses, St. Patrick, the patron saint of the country of which the shamrock is the symbol, sports, the institution of Guinness.

249 The violin, or fiddle, as it is known, is one of the most important instruments in traditional Irish music.

250-251 The horse-racing circuit, the pub during a musical festival, and the crowded streets: There are many places and ways to celebrate Saint Patrick's Day.

GAELIC SPIRIT

An ancient country anchored by its traditions, Ireland has undergone a process of significant "rejuvenation" over the last few decades. Moreover, it has achieved this without compromising the nation's specific cultural identity. One characteristic of the Irish is their pride. They are proud of their land; in fact, surveys have identified the Irish as the European population with the closest ties to its homeland. The same spirit is seen in the Irish passion for sports, a passion, for example, with Gaelic football that explodes in the hard-fought matches staged every Sunday at Croke Park Stadium in Dublin. The variety of the Irish landscape actually encourages sport, making the country a Mecca for lovers of golf, hiking, cycling, and horse racing, for example. Thousands of enthusiasts celebrate these activities at fêtes and festivals of an international standing. One example is the Irish National Hunt Festival held at Punchestown in County Kildare, one of the country's greatest race meetings. However, Ireland's calendar of events is highly diversified and is enriched by religious celebrations — the most eagerly awaited of which is undoubtedly St. Patrick's Day, March 17, dedicated to the country's patron saint. There are also festivals of music (including the Wexford Opera and Cork Jazz festivals), literature (such as Dublin's Bloomsday), and fine food and drink (such as the International Oyster Festival held at Clarinbridge in County Galway). Ireland is a land of ancient flavors. Rather than traditional recipes and dishes, however, these flavors are generally those of local whiskeys and beers (Guinness, first and foremost) that are veritable institutions here. The history of Irish whiskey and beer is as old as that of one of the most authentic "monuments" of Irish culture: the pub. The country has more than 11,000 pubs, and since time immemorial, in Dublin just as in the smallest, farthest-flung village, pubs have been the setting for one of Ireland's best-loved rituals: meeting friends, listening to old songs, and drinking a glass of good black stout or downing a shot of the "water of life." Beer, whiskey, and music are, in fact, the foundations and the pub itself the place of congregation. Once the custodian of traditional Irish music, the pub has proven to be an ideal showcase for groups that have progressed from performing in front of a local audience to the international stage. If it is true that the most innovative European rock music, such as that produced by groups of the caliber of U2, was born in Ireland (in the pubs of Dublin, to be precise), it is also just as true that in the eleventh and twelfth centuries

Irish harpists were already famous for the style of their compositions. The influence of continental Europe subsequently led to the introduction of other instruments and new sounds. Accordions, Irish harps, guitars, mandolins, wooden flutes and tin whistles, fiddles and bodhrans are traditional instruments that accompany Irish ballads today, and it is significant that echoes of ancient melodies can still be heard in contemporary music. Similarly, Ireland's literary heritage and its tormented history have, over recent decades, inspired the production of numerous films, with the country itself an ideal location capable of arousing a strong emotive impact.

252 TOP The famous "1000 Guineas" horse race is run at the Curragh in County Kildare.

252 BOTTOM Introduced to Ireland by the students of Trinity College, Dublin, rugby is now widely played.

253 TOP LEFT Windy Clew Bay is a favorite spot for sailors.

COMPETITION

AND IDENTITY

Ireland is by its very nature an ideal place for sports lovers. Blessed with infinite stretches of lush green fairway, the country is an Eden for golfers. Of about 400 courses, the most famous are to be found in County Kerry; among them is the renowned Ballybunion Golf Club, a uniquely attractive course set in the dunes overlooking the Atlantic Ocean. The Killarney Lakes area also boasts many fine courses and clubs; best known is the beautiful Killarney Golf Club. Walkers and cyclists are equally well served: Ireland offers a stunning range of rewarding itineraries and routes of varying physical demand. The Ring of Kerry, for example, winds through gentle mountains and along scenic shores in a circuit of about 180 km (110 miles) around the Iveragh Peninsula. It's a "once done, never forgotten" route. Ireland's big bays and small coves and its coastal waters attract hundreds of yachtsmen from all over the world. Many base themselves around Westport on Clew Bay, County Mayo, where the Atlantic offers great sailing. To the south, the entire coastline from the Dingle Peninsula east to Cork is dotted with bays and islands, and offers numerous challenging runs and safe anchorages. Horses and riding are almost a national obsession, an Irish passion deeply rooted in ancient popular traditions. Innumerable events confirm the bond between man and horse in Ireland: Throughout the year, festivals, horse fairs, and almost daily programs at the country's twenty-six racetracks draw large crowds. Among the principal racing events, mainly scheduled between April and October, are the Classic at the Curragh, the Powers Gold Label Irish Grand National, the Irish National Hunt, and the Irish Derby. Also not be missed are the great Galway, Listowel, Tralee, Killarney, and Punchestown festival events. Thanks to the Gaelic Athletic Association, a number of traditional Irish sports survive and enjoy strong support. They include hurling (perhaps best described as a combination of field and ice hockey), played for over 2,000 years. Two teams of fifteen players using curved sticks, or hurleys try to drive a leather ball, the *sliothar*, into their opponents' goal. There is also a women's version of hurling, called *camogie*, which is becoming increasingly popular. The most popular of the traditional Irish sports is Gaelic football, which resembles hurling in terms of its rules but is actually a combination of soccer and rugby. The most spectacular matches are organized at Croke Park in Dublin. Rugby, born in England in 1923, is now widely played.

253 TOP CENTER Hurling offers many spectacular moments.

253 TOP RIGHT Golf is the sport most suited to Ireland's green countryside.

253 BOTTOM Created by blending Celtic hurling and English rugby, Gaelic football is the sport that the Irish learn to love from early childhood.

254 AND 254-255 Gaelic football unites the formality of soccer with the cut-and-thrust of rugby. Either hands or feet may be employed in the game, and powerful and spectacular play results.

256-257 HURLING HAS AFFINITIES WITH BOTH HOCKEY AND SOCCER AND HAS BEEN PLAYED IN IRELAND FOR TWO THOUSAND YEARS. TWO TEAMS OF FIFTEEN PLAYERS FLING THE BALL WITH A CURVED STICK CALLED A "HURLEY."

258-259 IRELAND'S INTERNATIONAL RUGBY MATCHES ARE PLAYED IN DUBLIN'S LANSDOWNE ROAD STADIUM. THE TEAM IS DRAWN FROM BOTH NORTH AND SOUTH, AS THE GAME EMBRACES THE TWO TRADITIONS, AND IT NOW ENJOYS A GLORIOUS REPUTATION FOR SPORTSMANSHIP.

260-261 AND 262-263 MORE THAN A SPORT, HORSE RACING IS A PASSION. HORSES ARE THE
STARS OF MANY IRISH EVENTS, FESTIVALS, FAIRS AND, ABOVE ALL, RACES LIKE THOSE THAT HAVE
BEEN HELD AT LEOPARDSTOWN, DUBLIN, SINCE 1888.

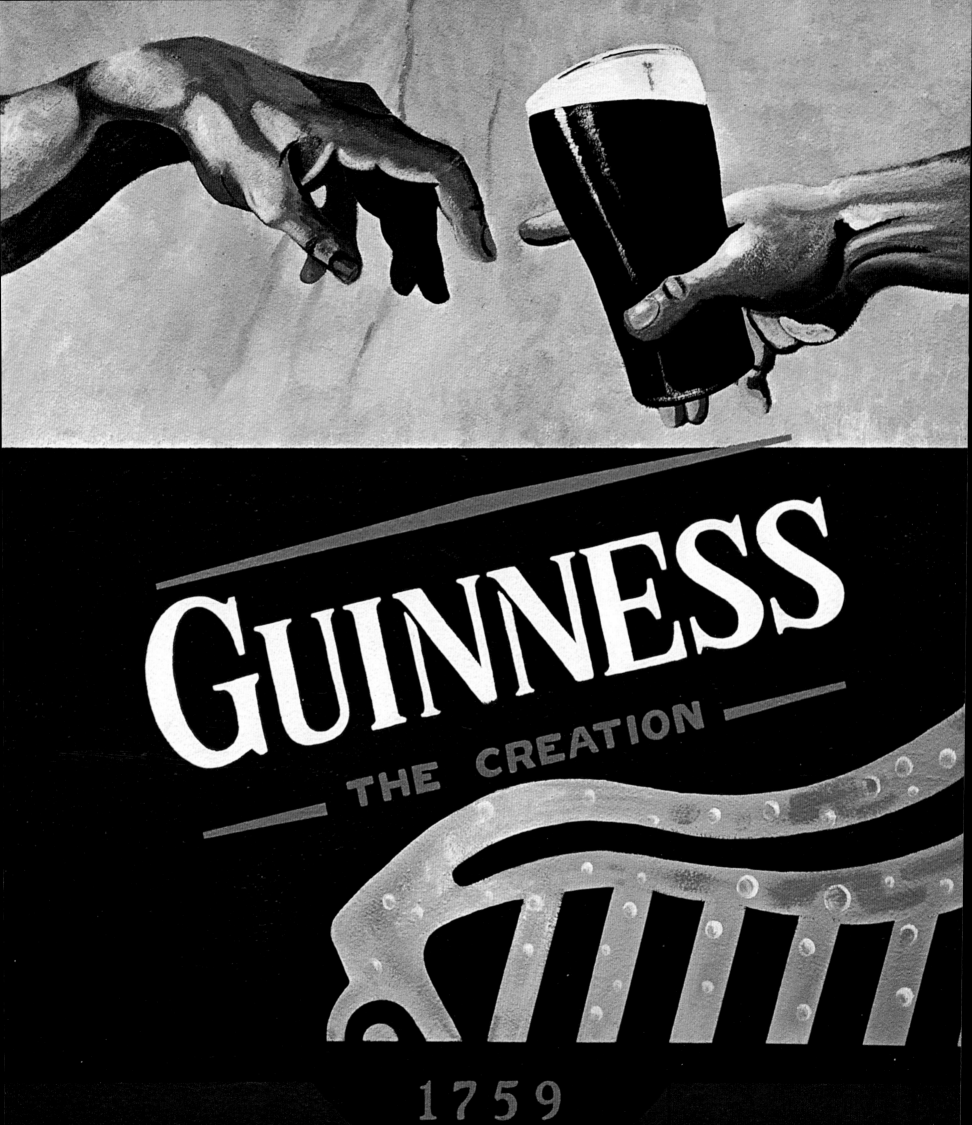

264 GUINNESS MAY NOT HAVE BEEN PART OF THE CREATION OF MAN, AS THIS IRONIC MURAL SUGGESTS, BUT IT HAS CERTAINLY SUCCEEDED IN MAKING ITSELF FAMOUS: GUINNESS IS THE MOST WIDELY KNOWN BEER IN THE WORLD.

265 TOP AND BOTTOM SOME GUINNESS-RELATED PLACES: THE MODERN GUINNESS FACTORY, A WALL DECORATED WITH AN AMUSING ADVERTISEMENT, AND THE UBIQUITOUS TRADITIONAL PUB.

GUINNESS

A NATIONAL INSTITUTION

As dark as stout, as light as lager or ale, as red as Smithwick's — as long as it's beer, the color is of little consequence. However, a truly dark color may well indicate Guinness, without doubt the queen of Irish beers. The history of this world-famous beer dates back to 1759. At that time, thirty-four-year-old Arthur Guinness, an enterprising young Dublin man who had learned to make beer from his father, Richard, decided to invest a small sum to rent the old St. James's Gate Brewery, a short distance from the River Liffey. The venture involved considerable risk: Irish breweries were in marked decline, and the only beer enjoying any success in the country was one called Entire, imported from England. This beer was originally known as "porter" because of its popularity among the porters of Billingsgate and Covent Garden, respectively London's fish and produce markets. Entire was a robust, black beer with a sweet aftertaste.

In his brew, Arthur used the same ingredients that went into porter (barley, hops, yeast, and water), but accentuated the bitterness of the hops, roasted the barley malt, and changed the quantity of yeast. What he came up with eventually became known as stout, an even darker

beer with a thick, creamy head. Guinness was born. The new beer was such a success that it soon began to be exported. Today it is available in various forms: Draught, a light stout with a smoky flavor; Extra Stout, with a ruby-black color and a bitter flavor; the stronger Foreign Extra Stout specially brewed for export; and Special Export with the highest alcohol content, brewed specifically for the Belgian market. Over the course of two centuries, Arthur Guinness's small brewery expanded to the point where it is now the largest in Europe, and the company founded by the astute Irishman now employs 3,000 people and produces around 3.5 million glasses of beer a day. The product is exported to 120 countries throughout the world and it is estimated that 10 million glasses of Guinness are drunk every day. Guinness has become a veritable institution in Ireland. This is demonstrated by the fact that in Crane Street in the Liberties area of Dublin, a museum has been dedicated to the beer: the Guinness Storehouse. Housed in a nineteenth-century building, the museum documents the evolution of the production process from its primitive beginnings to the adoption of twenty-first-century technology.

266-267 COMIC FIGURES AND CURIOUS ANIMALS FEATURE IN THE MANY MURALS INSPIRED BY GUINNESS, AND COLOR THE WALLS OF IRISH PUBS WITH THEIR IRONY.

268-269 THE LINK BETWEEN THE IRISH AND THEIR CULTURE IS VERY STRONG TODAY, AS INDICATED BY THE CASKS OF GUINNESS STACKED BENEATH A AN IRISH-LANGUAGE SIGN.

GUINNESS
FOR STRENGTH

CANTWELLS

MY GOODNESS

MY GUINNESS

GUINNESS

A CUR INA BAN AIR

THE WATER

OF LIFE

With or without the *e*? There is no room for doubt: If it is Irish, not Scottish, then it is spelled "whiskey." Whiskey can rightly be termed the "water of life," as the original Gaelic words for the much-loved distillate, *uisce beatha,* mean just that. Popular history suggests that the earliest distillers were Irish monks back in the sixth century. It is not only the extra vowel that distinguishes Irish whiskey from Scotch. The different manufacturing processes infuse distinctly different flavors to the two spirits. Irish whiskey is distilled a number of times (at least three) and the malt employed is dried in closed ovens to prevent contact with smoke. Casks formerly containing bourbon, port, or sherry are then used. This process, along with the aging period (at least three years), determines the final flavor. On Bow Street in Dublin visitors are welcome at the Irish Whiskey Corner, a museum dedicated to the production of the much-appreciated beverage. Housed in rooms in a wing of the former Jameson's distillery, the museum's exhibit leads visitors through the history of the distillation of Irish whiskey from small-scale distillation in sixth-century monasteries to high-volume production in the modern

Midleton plant, while explaining each step in process. The visit also includes a stop at the Ball O'Malt Bar for whiskey tasting. The vast Irish Distillers' plant at Midleton in County Cork comprises a number of different distilleries producing various brands of Irish whiskey. These include Jameson's and Tullamore Dew, aged in oak casks for between four and seven years. The visitors' route also includes the mills, maltings, ovens, granaries, and warehouses.

Among the other attractions there is the world's largest pot-still; it can hold up to 115,000 liters (30,000 gallons). Visitors end their tour in a special tasting room where they can sample various brands and see if they can tell which are Irish whiskey and which are Scotch. While Midleton is the largest Irish distillery, the oldest in the country and, indeed, in the world, is the Old Bushmills Distillery, on the outskirts of the town of Bushmills, in County Antrim. The distillery's "Grant to Distill" was issued in 1608, though it is likely that production predated permission by 200 years. Another typically Irish beverage associated with whiskey is Irish coffee, a blend of whiskey, sugar, and hot coffee topped with a layer of fresh cream, served in a tall warm glass.

271 TOP Many long-established distilleries can be visited today, like Old Bushmills, which has produced whiskey since 1608.

271 BOTTOM There are more than 15 Irish whiskeys. These bottles make a fine sight as they wait for someone to order a pint and a chaser — a beer and a whiskey to wash it down.

272 AND 273 An age-old dispute sets Irish whiskey against Scotch whisky. In fact, the two vary by more than just the spelling: the production processes are also different. Unlike Scotch whisky, Irish whiskey is produced with malt dried without smoking and is distilled several times in huge stills. At the end of the process, the liquid is stored in oak barrels for at least three years.

274 MUSIC LIES AT THE SOUL OF IRELAND AND THE TRADITIONAL FORMS CREATE A BOND BETWEEN THE GENERATIONS.

275 **TOP LEFT** THE CELTIC HARP HAS BEEN USED SINCE THE 10TH CENTURY AND IS THE ESSENCE OF IRISH MUSIC.

MUSIC

THE ESSENCE OF LIFE

Music is the epitome of Irish artistic creativity and national pride, and the country has a rich and a variegated musical heritage. In order to reconstruct the history of Irish music it's necessary to wind the clocks back many centuries. As early as the eleventh and twelfth centuries, the bards employed by the aristocratic courts of Ireland were composing heroic, chivalrous poems that were sung to the accompaniment of a harp. The Celtic harp, it should be remembered, is one of the musical instruments that, along with the flute, fiddle, accordion, and bodhrán (a goatskin drum), has never lost its appeal over the centuries. Even today the harp is often a feature of the myriad gigs held daily in the streets and pubs of Ireland. In the seventeenth century, even earlier than the famous ballads (stories told in song), lullabies, joyous airs, and laments (*suantraí, geantraí* and *goltraí* in Gaelic), were already very popular. In the eighteenth century, set dancing constituted the most popular form of folk dance and was based on military dances adapted to various musical instruments. The nineteenth and twentieth centuries saw many Irish composers achieve international success: Sir Charles Villiers Stanford (1852–1924) and Sir Hamilton Harty (1879–1941), for example, while the tenor John McCormack (1884–1945) was particularly popular in the United States. In recent times, certainly from the 1960s on, Irish folk music has been kept alive by groups such as the Dubliners, a historic band born in the pubs; the legendary Chieftains, led by Paddy Moloney; and Moving Hearts, a band fusing traditional Irish music with rock, blues, and jazz. Also important are Clannad, who combine folk and new age music, and the Pogues. Another of Irish music's legends is Van Morrison, Belfast's king of the blues. The list is extensive, enriched with numerous female vocalists of talent: from the torments of the highly original rock-pop artist Sinead O'Connor to the poetic Enya and Dolores O'Riordan, singer with the Cranberries. The most famous band is, however, composed of Bono, the Edge, Adam Clayton and Larry Mullen, Jr.: U2, one of the most successful rock groups of the last twenty years.

275 **TOP RIGHT AND BOTTOM**
LIVE MUSIC IN THE WARMTH OF PUBS ANYWHERE CAN CREATE A JOYFUL AND SOCIAL ATMOSPHERE.

276-277 A GROUP OF MUSICIANS IN A PUB IN GALWAY WITH THE INSTRUMENTS OF TRADITIONAL MUSIC: THE FIDDLE, ACCORDION, AND BODHRAN (A DRUM MADE WITH GOAT HIDE).

278 TOP U2, THE WORLD-FAMOUS BAND THAT BEGAN IN DUBLIN AT THE START OF THE 1980S, IS TYPICAL OF IRELAND'S MUSICAL VIVACITY AND EXPERIMENTATION WITH FORMS OTHER THAN FOLK MUSIC AND TRADITIONAL BALLADS.

278 BOTTOM THE DEEPLY ROOTED MUSICAL CULTURE OF IRELAND IS REFLECTED IN THE URBAN LANDSCAPE: THE WALLS OF WINDMILL LANE STUDIOS IN DUBLIN ARE COVERED WITH GRAFFITI EULOGIZING FAVORITE ARTISTS.

279 BONO (PAUL HEWSON) IS U2'S SINGER AND LEADER. HE IS ALSO KNOWN INTERNATIONALLY FOR HIS COMMITMENT TO SOCIAL PROGRESS AND HIS INVOLVEMENT IN CAMPAIGNS ON BEHALF OF DEVELOPING COUNTRIES. ON VARIOUS OCCASIONS HE HAS USED THE STAGE TO RAISE AWARENESS OF THESE THEMES AMONG THE PUBLIC.

A YEAR
OF FESTIVALS

Musical, literary, sporting, gastronomic, popular, or religious: The calendar of events and festivals marking the seasons in Ireland is both crowded and varied. Among the most eagerly awaited and the closest to Irish hearts is undoubtedly St. Patrick's Day, celebrated on March 17, when every Irish city and town organizes religious ceremonies, shows, and parades. The day is not only a national occasion, it is one that brings together Irish communities throughout the world. St. Patrick's Day is celebrated in cities from New York to Sydney, and, in each, costumes and allegorical floats commemorate the life of the saint. In the summer Ireland's innumerable religious sites become destinations for pilgrimages. Among the most grueling is the one to little Station Island in Lough Derg, to the southeast of Donegal, which takes place between June 1 and August 15. Station Island is where St. Patrick is said to have had a vision of purgatory while he spent forty days praying and fasting in order to rid Ireland of evil spirits. Pilgrims spend three days barefoot, subsisting on a single daily meal of bread and tea, and attending an all-night vigil.

On the last Sunday of July, on Croagh Patrick Mountain to the west of Westport, devotees of St. Patrick climb barefoot along a steep scree slope to the point where the saint is said to have rid Ireland of snakes for all eternity. Dublin offers a less rigorous observation; its annual St. Patrick's Festival puts on street theater, music, fireworks, and entertainment of all kinds. In June, the

capital is the setting for the Bloomsday Festival that celebrates James Joyce's *Ulysses* and explores the places associated with the life and personal dramas of the author and his much-studied Leopold Bloom.

Throughout the year, all over Ireland, horses and jockeys are the draw in numerous daily race meetings, horse fairs and racing festivals. At the top of the list is the fashionable Dublin Horse Show, which each August attracts thousands of enthusiasts from every corner of the globe.

The national capital puts talent to work and during the first two weeks of October hosts the Dublin Theatre Festival, and that same month, the Dublin City Marathon is run.

The Kilkenny Arts Festival, held in August, is this city's most eagerly awaited cultural event and its annual week in the news. Over a number of days the program offers jazz and classical music concerts, visual arts events, poetry and literature readings, open-air productions of Shakespeare, and exhibitions in the town's galleries and streets. In the northwest, medieval Galway is home to a very different event, the mouthwatering International Oyster Festival that in late September attracts hundreds of participants and onlookers to the town.

The foregoing is no more than a sample of offerings from Ireland's varied festival calendar. Those who attend an event invariably find they can couple it with fine dining and first-class scenic touring.

284 AND 285 Green is the dominant color at the St. Patrick's Day festival. It is clearly linked with the shamrock, an attribute of the saint since the 5th century, when he used it to illustrate the Christian concept of the Holy Trinity to the warlike Celts. Even young children are involved in the St. Patrick's Day festivities.

286 EQUESTRIAN SPORTS ENTHUSIASTS FLOCK TO THE ROYAL DUBLIN SOCIETY HORSE SHOW: IT OFFERS FIVE BUSY DAYS OF NATIONAL AND INTERNATIONAL COMPETITIONS.

286-287 A PANEL OF JUDGES AND GUESTS WATCHES THE OPENING CEREMONY AT THE ROYAL DUBLIN SOCIETY HORSE SHOW, ONE OF THE MOST POPULAR EVENTS OF THE DUBLIN SUMMER.

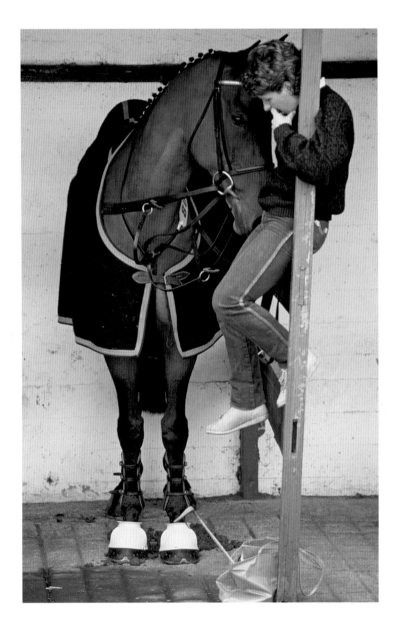

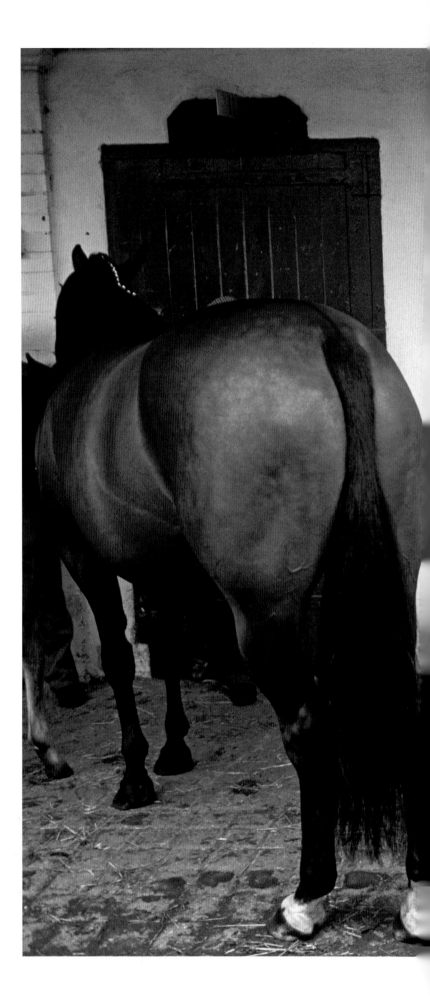

288 AND 289 The horses are the protagonists at the Royal Dublin Society Horse Show. Each year about 1,500 splendid stallions, mares, foals, and ponies take part in the many shows and jumping competitions.

290 The Dublin Horse Show is held in the Royal Dublin Society Showground and is the chance for the country's many horse-breeders to show off their animals to potential buyers.

290-291 A rider prepares to leave the stalls to take part in the competitions. Specific areas are reserved for each category of horse, as is shown by the sign at the back of the stable.

MEDIUM WEIGHT
HUNTERS

244

292 AND 293 THE PONIES HAVE A CLASS TO THEMSELVES IN THE DUBLIN HORSE SHOW. YOUNG AND VERY YOUNG RIDERS CAN TAKE PART IN JUMPING COMPETITIONS THAT OFTEN DO NOT DIFFER VERY MUCH FROM THOSE OF THEIR OLDER COLLEAGUES.

294 AND 295 THE DUBLIN HORSE SHOW IS A SOCIAL EVENT THAT DRAWS THE MEMBERS OF IRELAND'S HIGH SOCIETY. HERE ARE TWO SEASONED SPECTATORS WEARING ELEGANT OUTFITS SUITED TO THE OCCASION.

INDEX

PHOTO CREDITS

ANTONIO ATTINI/ARCHIVIO WHITE STAR: pages 4-5, 58 top right, 58 bottom left, 59, 61 top left, 61 bottom, 62, 63 bottom, 65 left, 65 right, 68 bottom, 76-77, 78-79, 88-89, 90-91, 96, 97 top left, 97 top right, 98, 99, 102-103, 106-107, 108-109, 111, 126-127, 128-129, 130, 132-133, 134-135, 138 left, 138 right, 146 left, 170-171, 197 left, 199 right, 228 left, 228 right.

LIVIO BOURBON/ARCHIVIO WHITE STAR: pages 1, 58 top left, 58 bottom right, 61 top right, 68 left, 68 right, 69, 70-71, 72-73, 74 bottom, 75, 80, 80-81, 82-83, 125,

131, 136 bottom right, 138 center, 139 top, 140 center, 140 right, 145 center, 145 right, 146 center, 147 left, 147 center, 148, 149 bottom, 162, 163, 166-167, 168-169, 170, 172-173, 173, 176, 176-177, 178, 178-179, 182, 188-189, 197 center, 197 right, 198, 199 left, 199 center, 202-203, 204, 212, 216, 217, 218, 219, 220, 221, 222, 223, 226, 227, 228 center, 230, 236, 237 top right, 238, 239, 240-241, 242, 243 left, 243 center, 243 bottom, 245, 246, 264, 265 top.

GIULIO VEGGI/ARCHIVIO WHITE STAR: pages 11, 100-101, 145 bottom, 146 right, 147 right,

167, 174-175, 248 bottom right, 252 top center, 252 bottom, 275 top right.

ABBAS/MAGNUM PHOTOS/ CONTRASTO: page 209.

AISA: pages 21 left, 32-33, 33 right.

JON ARNOLD/JON ARNOLD IMAGES/ALAMY IMAGES: page 157 right.

ADRIANO BACCHELLA: page 281 top left.

TOM BEAN/CORBIS/ CONTRASTO: pages 94-95.

BETTMANN/CORBIS/ CONTRASTO: pages 34 right, 38 bottom, 48 left, 57 center.

TIBOR BOGNAR/CORBIS/ CONTRASTO: page 243 right.

PATRICK BOLGER/INPHO: pages 14-15, 257, 262-263.

BRIDGEMAN ART LIBRARY: pages 22, 24 left, 33 left, 54 left.

JOHN COGILL STRINGER/ ASSOCIATED PRESS: pages 251 right, 282-283.

CONOR CAFFREY: page 284 bottom.

DAVE CAULKIN/ASSOCIATED PRESS: pages 258-259

STEFANO CELLAI/SIE: page 280.

300 FALLING SOMEWHERE BETWEEN THE SPONTANEOUS AND THE INSPIRED, THIS
PAINTING OF A WOMAN WITH A DRINK (PROBABLY A PINT OF STOUT) ADORNS THE
EXTERIOR OF A PUB IN LIMERICK. IRELAND HAS A STRONG ATTACHMENT TO
ITS IDENTITY EVEN IN ITS DRINKS; THE TRADITION FOR CENTURIES HAS BEEN
TO DRINK BEER BREWED IN IRELAND.

Thunder Bay Press
An imprint of the Advantage Publishers Group
5880 Oberlin Drive, San Diego, CA 92121-4794
www.thunderbaybooks.com

Copyright © 2003 White Star S.r.l.

Translation: Neil Davenport and Timothy Stroud

notations of errors or omissions should
be addressed to Thunder Bay Press,
Editorial Department, at the address at
left. All other correspondence (author
inquiries, permissions) concerning the
content of this book should be addressed
to White Star S.r.l., Via C. Sassone, 22/24,
13100 Vercelli, Italy, www.whitestar.it.

ISBN 1-59223-103-9

Printed in Italy
1 2 3 4 5 07 06 05 04 03

Library of Congress Cataloging-in-Publication
Data available upon request.